PRAISE FOR

Good Night, Lord

Quin Sherrer captures the hearts of women of all ages as she shares
from her life's experiences to help women reach their destiny. Her
love for women shines through to give hope and encouragement in
their daily walk with God. The prayers at the end of each devotional
are simple yet profound and reflect the heart of God.

BETH ALVES
INTERCESSORS INTERNATIONAL
BULVERDE, TEXAS

Quin Sherrer's *Good Night, Lord* is stimulating reading. She expertly
tells stories of friends, and very delicately weaves in stories of her own
family that will bring life to many struggling women.

BOBBYE BYERLY
DIRECTOR OF PRAYER AND INTERCESSION
WORLD PRAYER CENTER
COLORADO SPRINGS, COLORADO

Good Night, Lord is a book of powerful insights and tender prayers.
Quin Sherrer gently reminds us of our faithful God who cares deeply
about our hopes, our joys, our   · day.

ALI
AUTHOR OF *S*
REDM

D1280199

Quin Sherrer simply and eloquently helps women to understand our
utter, everyday dependence upon a God who answers prayer. She
demonstrates that nothing is too big—or too small—to bring to the
Lord. His love for us shines through these pages.

ESTHER S. ILNISKY
ESTHER NETWORK INTERNATIONAL
CHILDREN'S GLOBAL PRAYER MOVEMENT
WEST PALM BEACH, FLORIDA

Good Night, Lord is one of the most comforting books I have ever read. If you have children of any age, it will be a great blessing to you. The pages seem to open up and embrace you with the love of God.

CINDY JACOBS
COFOUNDER, GENERALS OF INTERCESSION
COLORADO SPRINGS, COLORADO

Quin Sherrer, with her lovable transparency, welcomes us into her walk with God. You will find here humor, wisdom and truths for life. You may want to *start* each day with this book.

MIRIAM NEFF
AUTHOR AND COUNSELOR
CHICAGO, ILLINOIS

Good Night, Lord radiates with the warmth of a mother's heart. Quin Sherrer, a spiritual mother to a multitude of praying women around the world, will take you by the hand and lead you on a private journey through the pages of her heart and the stages of her life. You will both witness and be challenged to experience a life of intimacy with the Father.

ALICE SMITH
PRAYER COORDINATOR, U.S. PRAYER TRACK
HOUSTON, TEXAS

INSPIRATION FOR THE END OF THE DAY

Good Night, LORD

QUIN SHERRER

Regal

A Division of Gospel Light
Ventura, California, U.S.A.

Published by Regal Books
A Division of Gospel Light
Ventura, California, U.S.A.
Printed in U.S.A.

Regal Books is a ministry of Gospel Light, an evangelical Christian publisher dedicated to serving the local church. We believe God's vision for Gospel Light is to provide church leaders with biblical, user-friendly materials that will help them evangelize, disciple and minister to children, youth and families.

It is our prayer that this Regal book will help you discover biblical truth for your own life and help you meet the needs of others. May God richly bless you.

For a free catalog of resources from Regal Books/Gospel Light please call your Christian supplier, or contact us at 1-800-4-GOSPEL.

Cover Design by Kevin Keller
Interior Design by Rob Williams
Edited by Deena Davis

Library of Congress Cataloging-in-Publication Data

Sherrer, Quin.
    Good night, Lord / Quin Sherrer.
      p. cm.
    Includes bibliographical references.
    ISBN 0-8307-2523-7
      1. Christian women—Religious life. 2. Women—Prayer-books and devotions. I. Title.

BV4527 .S4245 2000   99-059085
242'.643—dc21

1 2 3 4 5 6 7 8 9 10 11 12 13 14 15 / 05 04 03 02 01 00

Rights for publishing this book in other languages are contracted by Gospel Literature International (GLINT). GLINT also provides technical help for the adaptation, translation and publishing of Bible study resources and books in scores of languages worldwide. For further information, contact GLINT, P.O. Box 4060, Ontario, CA 91761-1003, U.S.A. You may also send e-mail to Glintint@aol.com, or visit their website at www.glint.org.

CONTENTS

Acknowledgments 9

Introduction: A Woman's Field of Influence 11

PART ONE
PRAYING THROUGH ORDINARY DAYS

Waiting Prayers 21

A Christian Home 23

No One at My Table 25

Peace to This House 27

At Least Once a Week 29

Mealtime Blessings 31

Traditions 34

Honor to Moms 36

A Lesson in Ink 39

Going Home to Mother's 41

His Voice Gently Speaks 43

Company's Coming 45

Ode to a Garage 47

Marriage-Go-Round 49

Out-of-the-Ordinary Days 51

Career and Motherhood 53

Letter to a First Grader 55

Get Out of His Way 57

My Hope with His Frog 60

My Last First Grader 62

An Extra Child to Love 64

A Child's Mentor 67

What Will I Be? 70

Unconditional Love 73

A Mother's Desire 75

Praying Grandparents 77

Anyone Home? 80

Bless the Grands 81

The Next Generation 83

Need a Miracle? 85

Sour Days Turn Sweet 87

Another Woman 88

Reaching Her Neighbors 89

A Mutual Friend 91

Five Blessings 93

Pass the Prayer Mantle 95

PART TWO
PRAYING THROUGH BATTLE DAYS

Remember Roses 103

Boundaries and Balance 104

Avoiding Pitfalls 106

Saying No to Addictions 109

Dealing with Low Self-Esteem 111

Fear Versus Faith 114

Keep an Eye on the Ark 116

God's Timing 119

Life's Rhythm with Balance 122

Be Prepared 124

Sin Always Affects Others 126

Our Military Personnel 128

Spiritual Weapons of Authority 130

Safeguard Your Home 132

Prayers for Our Children 134

Me, a Coward? 138

Something to Cherish 140

Stretcher Bearer for God 143

Releasing a Friend on Earth 145

Prayerwalking 147

Praying for Unsaved Friends 150

Broken Marriage 152

Dying Without the Savior 153

Call for Help 155

God Longs to Speak to Us 157

Neighborhood, City and Nation 160

A Significant Time 163

Aim on Target 166

PART THREE
EXPERIENCING VICTORY DAYS

When Our Mountain Moved 171

Roots and Heritage 175

Legacy of Love 178

Give Children to God 180

My Promise Shell 183

Prodigals Come Home 186

Covenant-Keeping God 188

In an Instant 190

You Are Him Here 193

In Remembrance of Him 195

Praying for a Dying Stranger 197

A Voice from the Past 199

Another Birthday 201

Who Are Your Friends? 203

Prized Prayer Partners 206

The News Speaks 209

A Stranger Blesses My Day 211

Applying the Blood 213

Forgiveness Is a Choice 215

Taken for Granted 217

People or Things? 219

A Dream Fulfilled 221

How to Reach Them? 223

One Mother's Idea 225

God's Embroidery 227

Leaving a Prayer Legacy 230

He Is Not Here 232

No Bread from Stone 234

Please Pray with Me 236

Dream House 238

Full Circle 241

What's the Takeaway? 244

ACKNOWLEDGMENTS

I wish to bless and thank Bob Hudson, editor emeritus of the *Star Advocate* newspaper, Titusville, Florida, for allowing me to be a reporter, feature writer and columnist for him in my early journalism days. Best of all, he let me work so that I was home when my children were out of school. He gave me exciting and satisfying assignments—interviewing astronauts and celebrities who came to the space launches, covering all 16 local schools and writing features on people in their everyday walks of life. One day I asked if I could write more about how faith in Jesus changes lives in our community. He gave me a full page every Friday for a "religion" section. Not only did I write personal testimonies, but my column "Good Night, Lord" was birthed. He was a rare boss. Thanks, Mr. Hudson.

I also thank my husband, LeRoy, and our three children, Quinett, Keith and Sherry, for their continued support of my writing career over the years. I pray that my grandchildren—Kara, Evangeline, Lyden Benjamin, Victoria Jewett and Samuel—will use the stories I've shared as a challenge to follow and serve God faithfully all their lives.

To Deena Davis, my editor, and Regal's Kyle Duncan, Bill Greig III, Kim Bangs and Billie Baptiste, who believed in this book, a big THANKS.

To two pastors who greatly influenced my spiritual life—Pastor Peter Lord and Pastor Dutch Sheets. May God Himself reward you.

To you readers, I pray God will stir in you a desire to go to Him in prayer each night with whatever is on your heart. He's always waiting to listen, comfort, reassure and answer.

A Woman's Field

OF INFLUENCE

Every woman, at one time or another, ponders the question of her significance—we all want to make a difference in the lives of our families and the people God brings across our paths. We desire to have a positive, encouraging and uplifting effect on others.

The truth is, no woman's life is insignificant. Each of us has a specific sphere of influence and a unique journey God intends for us to take. With the different roles we assume and the ever-changing circumstances in which we find ourselves, the road changes.

Someone once said that every time you encounter another person, you both receive either a charge to or a drain on your spiritual battery. No one has a neutral effect on others. Each of us continually exerts influence—to bless or wound, to help or hurt. No matter how ordinary you may think your life (or how chaotic), you not only have a sphere of influence, but you also have the potential to move spiritual mountains through your consistent and persistent prayers for those you influence.

Over the years I've come to believe it is every woman's responsibility to recognize her field of influence, to tend and bless it, to defend it in prayer and, as a result, to experience the harvest God will bring.

My field of influence has changed with the seasons of my life. Yours will, too. Changes could include marriage, rearing children, a career, an empty nest, retirement, possible widowhood. But no matter how your field widens or narrows, you will have some type of influence over it.

Once when reading a passage of Scripture about one of David's mighty men, Shammah, whose name means "God is there," I was struck with the revelation that I as a woman had a field to defend in the spiritual realm. The story goes:

> When the Philistines [the enemy] banded together at a place where there was a field full of lentils [beans], Israel's troops fled from them. But Shammah took his stand in the middle of the field. He defended it and struck the Philistines down, and the LORD brought about a great victory (2 Sam. 23:11,12).

While Shammah took his stand to defend his bean patch—his turf—*it was the Lord who brought the victory*. So it is with us. When we are faithful to pray for those people for whom God has called us to intercede, He brings about the victory. Maybe not in our expected time frame and surely not always in the ways we envision, but always for our good and His ultimate glory.

DEFENDING YOUR BEAN PATCH

At the beginning of time, God put man in the Garden of Eden to tend, guard and keep watch over it (see Gen. 2:15). This Scripture is significant because it is the first mention of watching over. God wants us to keep the enemy out of the territory He has entrusted to us—to guard the boundaries of the field as watchmen in the Bible did.

Defending my bean patch consists of praying for my family, friends, extended family, neighborhood, city, nation and the country God puts on my heart. Your field will vary from mine, but we pray for some of the same things as the Lord leads us: for blessings (physical and financial), for direction, protection, provision and, if the people we pray for don't know the Lord, for salvation.

When I pray, I've learned to be explicit in my requests and persistent in bringing them before God. I've found that praying with prayer partners has enhanced my prayer life. I call it the "prayer of agreement."

I have discovered the hard way that I can't pray with obstacles in my heart: no unbelief, no unforgiveness and no unconfessed sin. I'm learning—always learning—new ways to pray for my field, but it's only through the leading of the Holy Spirit that I can know my prayers are aligned with God's will.

So often we forget who we are and to whom we belong. By reaffirming what God's Word says about us we can drive away every dark doubt. Agreeing with the Word of God is a sure way to gain victory over insecurities, feelings of inferiority and low self-image. Here's what God's Word says about you:

God is at work in you to will and work for His good pleasure (see Phil. 2:13).

The Lord knows everything about you. He knows when you sit and when you rise; He perceives your thoughts before you ever give them words. He is familiar with all your ways (see Ps. 139: 1-3; read verses 13-18).

The Lord will fulfill his purpose for you (see Ps. 138:8).

You are his workmanship [handiwork] created in Christ Jesus for good works, which God prepared beforehand that you should do them (see Eph. 2:10).

If you have accepted Christ, you are God's daughter—a King's daughter, clothed in strength and dignity (see Prov. 31:25, *TLB*). *Strength* is the quality of being strong—the capacity to sustain force without yielding or breaking. *Dignity* is the quality of being stately; it is nobility of manner; it is the quality of being excellent, worthy or honorable. Women who follow Christ are powerful women—persons of strength, might, authority and ability.

As we take our places where God has planted us, becoming watchmen for that field and focusing our trust on Him, we can be sure He will direct our lives and our intercession.

One writer put it this way:

> You may not think your little field is very important. But God has set you in your field as a watchman. Most of us don't realize it, but our sphere of influence is much larger than we can ever imagine—and will continue on for generations to come, be it good or evil. It's a wonderful responsibility—frightening at times—but wonderful. Always remember, though, you're never in your watchtower alone. Jesus is ever with you and His Spirit will whisper just the things you need to say and do.[1]

It is my prayer that before you are finished reading this book, you will desire to live intentionally and with a God-given sense of destiny in your bean patch—your field of influence. By doing so, you will make an eternal difference!

Lord, thank You that You consider me special, significant, a woman with a purpose. Thank You that You will begin to show me more specifically what my field of influence is so that I can pray with greater sensitivity. I want my prayers to be breathed by Your Holy Spirit. I am so glad I'm Your daughter. Thank You, Lord. Amen.

Note
1. Jamie Buckingham, *The Nazarene* (Ann Arbor, Mich.: Servant Publications, 1991), p. 89.

PART ONE

Praying Through
ORDINARY DAYS

When you end the day and you want to say "Good night, Lord," how do you express what's really on your heart? I found myself in that position when I was a busy younger mom just starting to write down my prayers in a journal. I didn't know it then, but I was forming the habit of giving every day to God.

Some of those prayers are recorded here, beginning with the time when my children were young and progressing to my role as a grandmother of five today. The stories I've included with the prayers deal with issues common to every woman's life. Hopefully, some of the incidents I describe will encourage you to rely on God through the ups and downs of your own life.

Raised by a single working mom, I know firsthand what it's like to help care for three younger siblings, to help run a boarding house, to work two jobs to go to school and later to rear three children of my own (all born in less than four years). It is in this type of environment, the home, that our greatest spiritual battles are fought and won.

ON AN ORDINARY AFTERNOON

Corrie ten Boom used to say, "Our everyday life is our battle place."[1] It is often the day-in, day-out events of life that provide some of the biggest opportunities to pray what's on our hearts. It is also when we need to remain the most alert. For instance, we need to be on guard *in our minds*: the devil will attempt to plant thoughts in our minds that don't agree with truth as found in God's Word. We need to be on guard *in our hearts*—against attitudes and emotions that will give the devil a foothold in our lives. And we need to be on guard *with our mouths* against speaking unbelief, slander and sarcasm (see Ps. 141:3). You never know what an ordinary day might bring.

Every summer my friend Jackie (not her real name) traveled from her home in the South to attend her annual family reunion in the North. As one of few Christians in her extremely large family of siblings, aunts, uncles and cousins, she had prayed for the salvation of her family for many years.

Last summer she went to the reunion again. As they sat around visiting one afternoon, one of Jackie's sisters stood up and said, "These reunions are so nice that I think we should continue them someday in heaven. But we had all better be sure we're going to heaven. So, Jackie, would you come up here and pray with all of us, so we can go to heaven and get to come to other family reunions?"

Jackie was shocked but honored. She rose from her chair and stood beside her sister and began speaking: "Praying for salvation is special, but it isn't just so we can go to heaven. It's special for here on earth, too. Jesus came to give us abundant life. Salvation also includes healing, safety and protection. So will you all just pray out loud after me?

"Father, I come to You in the name of Jesus and admit I am in need of Your forgiveness, mercy, grace, peace . . ." As she continued leading them in a prayer to surrender their wills to His purposes, each person there repeated the prayer after her. In all, 40 of her relatives came to the Lord that day—a day that was seemingly little different from any other.

God is calling you to defend a specific bean patch comprising your family and all the other people He has placed within your field of influence. He wants you to keep that patch free from predators that would threaten their well-being. Your first line of defense is your willingness to take up the challenge to pray and then to rely on God for the outcome.

Yes, even on ordinary days it's important to remember to whom we belong: "Fear not, for I have redeemed you; I have summoned you by name; you are mine" (Isa. 43:1).

Note
1. Corrie ten Boom, *Marching Orders for the End Battle* (Ft. Washington, Penn.: Christian Literature Crusade, 1969), p. 23.

Waiting Prayers

I [Jesus] am telling you, whatever you ask for in prayer, believe (trust and be confident) that it is granted to you, and you will [get it].

MARK 11:24, AMP

I hate to admit it, but my early prayer life was more crisis-based than belief-based. When one of my children was headed to the emergency room, I would cry in panic, "Lord, do something, because I can't." Other times I prayed what I would call general "bless us" prayers.

Many years ago at a writer's conference, I was seated across the dinner table from Catherine Marshall, whom I'd long admired. I knew her reputation as an author and praying mother. I asked her, "Can you give me some advice on how to pray more effectively for my three children?"

She replied, "Be as specific in your prayers as you can and plant waiting prayers for your children's future." She told me she had prayed specifically for her son's future when he was still small; God had far exceeded what she had asked for. She called it "planting waiting prayers"—prayers that wouldn't be answered until some future date.

She also encouraged me to begin keeping a prayer journal, advising me to write down brief prayers and later to jot down how and when God had answered them.

Later that evening at the conference she challenged all of us with a startling question: "When you pray, do you really expect anything to happen?"

After I arrived home, I began to dig through the Bible to read everything I could find on prayer. Among other insights, I discovered that God is pleased with prayers of thanksgiving, petition, confession, praise and intercession. And sometimes He wants us to fast while we pray.

For more than 25 years now I have kept a prayer diary, journaling God's faithful answers. I've watched Him deal with each member of my family and gently bring three wandering youngsters back to Himself.[1] Not that all my requests have been granted! But as I have developed a closer intimacy with the Lord, I have come to understand that He wants the best for us.

GOOD NIGHT, LORD

Lord, how glad I am that You care about every detail of my life and the lives of my family. Thank You for Your faithfulness to us over the years. Forgive my times of doubt and unbelief. Forgive me for waiting until crisis times to come asking. Help me to trust You even as I wait for some long-ago breathed prayers to still be answered. I love You tonight, Lord, not so much for what You do for me but for who You are—a faithful Father. Amen.

Note
1. Quin Sherrer, *Miracles Happen When You Pray* (Grand Rapids, Mich.: Zondervan Publishing House, 1997), pp. 16, 17.

A Christian Home

She watches over the affairs of her household and
does not eat the bread of idleness.

PROVERBS 31:27

A woman's home has always been her greatest sphere of influence—even in Bible times, when the Hebrew mother shared the responsibility with the father for training her children and expressed the gift of hospitality.

> After the destruction of the Temple in Jerusalem and the scattering of the Jewish nation into exile, the rabbis referred to the home as a small sanctuary or miniature temple.... The home, like the Temple, was to be set aside for the worship of God, a house of study to learn the Torah, and the serving of the community needs.... Each home was to reflect God's glory through prayer and praise.[1]

Anne Ortlund believes that a Christian home is a powerful "show-and-tell." She writes: "Through the years, Christian homes have won more Christian converts than all preachers and teachers put together."[2]

Your home is God's provision for you. It can be a blessing to others and a tool of ministry to the people God sends your way. But there is no one—absolutely no one—more important to serve and love than the very family God has placed in your home.

We have had a special plaque hanging in our kitchen for years. Its words represent the principles we hold most dear as a family:

God Made Us a Family

We need one another.
We love one another.
We forgive one another.
We work together.
We play together.
We worship together.
Together we use God's Word.
Together we grow in Christ.
Together we love all men.
Together we serve our God.
Together we hope for heaven.
These are our hopes and ideals;
Help us to attain them, O God;
Through Jesus Christ our Lord, Amen.[3]

Lord, once again I make this my prayer. Amen.

Notes
1. Marvin R. Wilson, *Our Father Abraham: Jewish Roots of the Christian Faith* (Grand Rapids, Mich.: Eerdmans, 1989), pp. 214, 215.
2. Anne Ortlund, *Disciplines of the Home* (Dallas: Word, 1990), p. 41.
3. "The Christian Family Standard," adopted by the Family Life Committee of the Lutheran Church, Missouri Synod. Quoted in *Helping Families Through the Church* (St. Louis: Concordia, 1957), n.p.

No One at My Table

The King will reply, "I tell you the truth, whatever you did for one of the least of these brothers of mine, you did for me."

MATTHEW 25:40

For 10 years my mother operated a boarding house in Tallahassee, Florida, to help support and educate her four children. I was the oldest. Because she served family style—all you could eat for 75 cents—each day she fed between 300 and 600 college boys, construction crews, state legislature workers and teachers.

My sister and I had to wait tables, refilling tea glasses and bowls of piping hot vegetables. How I hated it. In fact, I made an inner vow I'd never have anyone at my table when I had a home of my own. After my marriage to LeRoy, a college boy who ate at my mother's Monroe Inn, I could envision only one man to feed all my life—only *one* man!

We moved to Houston where we both worked to get him through engineering school. In the almost three years we were there, I kept my inner vow by inviting only one other couple over for dessert. Definitely not for a meal.

We moved several more times, living in motels, a converted chicken shack, a mobile home. Finally we settled down in a small tract house near Kennedy Space Center in a city where we would live until LeRoy retired.

Now I was a young mother of three children under five years of age and I still did not know how to be hospitable. One day while we were visiting a new church meeting in the city library, Lib Parker introduced herself to me and invited us to Sunday lunch.

"Sorry, but I don't have enough to feed you," she said, as she introduced us to her husband, Gene, and their four little boys.

"But if you'd like to bring your lunch over, we could put it with ours and have plenty, I'm sure."

And that's what we did—at the Parker home one Sunday and at our house the next. For one year we shared our lunches and got comfortable having another family sitting at our table. Then we realized we were practicing hospitality. I was getting over my fear as a young homemaker about sharing what we had.

A few years later, I made a decisive step: I asked Jesus to be my Lord, not just my Savior. I invited the Holy Spirit to live in and through me. Suddenly, I wanted to have *lots* of people at our home. I wanted it to be a haven, a refuge, a place of security, a house of hospitality. By now we had moved from our small house to one with a lot more space.

I began to discover that the more Christ was at home in my heart, the more I wanted Him to be at home in my home.

I started to keep a guest book of those who visited. One week, 96 people had signed in; some came to eat, some to fellowship and some to stay overnight. I had long ago canceled my inner vow not to have anyone to our table.

GOOD NIGHT, LORD

Lord, sometimes I need to be reminded of the days when I was shy and unsure of myself around others, completely uneasy about having them in our home because I thought it had to be picture perfect. Help me to keep an open door to those You want to send my way. Amen.

Peace to This House

My people will live in peaceful dwelling places, in secure homes,
in undisturbed places of rest.

ISAIAH 32:18

Jesus told His disciples when they went into a town or village to search for a worthy person and stay at his house. "As you enter the home, give it your greeting. If the home is deserving, let your peace rest on it" (Matt. 10:12,13).

LeRoy and I had recently moved and we wanted our home to be deserving, to have that peace. We wanted to dedicate our home to the Lord in some manner. We invited a pastor friend from a liturgical church to lead us.

Kneeling at the coffee table in our living room, we acknowledged God's ownership of our home while the pastor recited a house blessing:

Let the almighty power of the Holy God be present in this place to banish from it every unclean spirit, to cleanse it from every residue of evil and to make it a secure habitation for those who dwell in it. In the name of Jesus Christ our Lord.

We went from room to room as he prayed in each, asking God's blessing on those who would use or occupy that room. Then he added, "And now, Lord, use this house for Your glory and this family to love others to You. Amen."

We have moved several times since our initial house-blessing ceremony. But in each dwelling we have had a dedication serv-ice—even in a small apartment on a Dallas Bible-school campus.

We didn't always have a pastor to help, so we would perform the ceremony ourselves with a few close friends as guests.

Dedication ceremonies with appropriate speeches were common in Israel's history. For example, Psalm 30 is a song sung at the dedication of the house of David. In Deuteronomy 20:5, the question is asked, "Has anyone built a new house and not dedicated it?" as though this was an expected action. Of course, the dedication of the house of God was celebrated with joy; read about it in Ezra 6:16.

One of the most important family values in Judaism is a peaceful home—it is called *shalom bayit*. Jesus taught, "Blessed are the peacemakers." A Christian home then, should be a peaceful home.

Have you thought of dedicating your home for God's purposes? Why not make it a special occasion, asking God to help make yours a house of many blessings! One thing I can guarantee: You will be blessed, all who enter your home will be blessed; and God will be glorified.

GOOD NIGHT, LORD

Thank You, Lord, for all the people You have allowed to come to our home. I pray that the hospitality offered them—whether just a meal or an overnight stay—brought refreshment to their bodies and their souls. May all others who come here feel the peace of the Lord. And may those of us who live here continue to know Your peace. Amen.

At Least Once a Week

Let us hold fast the confession of our hope without wavering, for He who promised is faithful; and let us consider how to stimulate one another to love and good deeds, not forsaking our own assembling together.

HEBREWS 10:23-25, *NASB*

The mother sits in church, viewing her freshly scrubbed and fairly neat family. She is thankful she made it on time this Sunday . . . again.

Just before they left the house, Sunny lost his favorite long red tie and didn't want a substitute. Three-year-old sister announced she would stay home by herself. The six-year-old, expecting to lose a tooth, didn't want to be in church when that happened. Dad waited until the last minute to polish his shoes.

No matter how early they get up, they can't seem to escape the last-minute rush. But for that once-a-week worship service, outside thoughts, worries and problems are laid aside. Their voices sing a song of praise. Their ears listen to words of wisdom read from the Holy Bible. Their hearts are open to receive the message of forgiveness, the promise of salvation through Jesus Christ.

It doesn't matter that the tie doesn't match or the shoes aren't shined or the tooth didn't come out. What matters is that this family finally made it to church to worship together and thank God for their blessings.

It matters that they remember to thank Him that they live in a free country where they may gather to worship as they please, that they have health and home and happiness, that they remember to pray for those less fortunate—those in need of food, medicine and shelter; those who are fighting in a war to preserve peace; and those separated from their families and loved ones.

It's important that in a year when the nation is bemoaning the high cost of living, wars in far-off countries, the lack of luxuries some yearn for, that they sing with dedicated fervor to the God of all blessings.

GOOD NIGHT, LORD

Lord, thank You for the effort families make to get to church to worship You. For some it is routine and traditional, yet others find it hard to get dressed and arrive on time. Help us be more concerned about worshiping You than wanting to impress others with the way we dress or smile or talk. Purify my heart, O Lord, that I may come to You with thanksgiving and praise for the blessings You have provided. Amen.

Mealtime Blessings

*Behold, I stand at the door and knock; if anyone hears My voice and opens the
door, I will come in to him, and will dine with him, and he with Me.*

REVELATION 3:20, *NASB*

Consider the significance of mealtimes at home with your family.
"The dinner table is the traditional symbol and practical center
of family togetherness," writes Dr. Paul Mickey. "It is the place
where we eat, talk, relax, and enjoy the company of those we love
most. . . . Every mealtime is a time of giving and receiving, serving and being served."[1]

"Someone has worked to pay for the food . . . shopped for the
food . . . prepared it . . . cleaned up the dining area and set the
table attractively. As the meal begins, someone will pass a dish to
you, and you will pass it on to someone else. Everyone is serving
and being served."[2]

Jesus revered the common meal. At His last meal with His
disciples He broke unleavened bread and shared the cup. We call
it The Lord's Supper. He went to a wedding; He dined with
Pharisees; He served dinner on the ground to more than 5,000
people. He, the Son of God, prepared breakfast for His disciples
by the Sea of Galilee after His resurrection.

On at least 20 occasions recorded in Scripture, Jesus partici-
pated in a meal or told a parable related to a mealtime experience.
He usually broke bread with His disciples at the end of the day.[3]

How sad that today's trend finds fewer families sitting down
to enjoy at least one meal together each day. The busyness of our
lives is part of the problem—all the after-school activities and the
fact that many parents work late at the office.

I remember the night I decided to make our mealtimes more
significant. I set the dining-room table with a beautiful cloth

and lighted candles and arranged a flower centerpiece. When the children came in to eat, they curiously poked their heads into the room.

"Who's coming for supper?" the youngest asked.

"You are!" I replied. "Because to me you are the most important people who will ever eat at our table." I shocked them. No more plastic tablecloth on the kitchen table with any old dishes I could find.

We continued that practice for years. I immediately noticed the blessings and benefits: We lingered longer to talk and share as we enjoyed the room previously reserved for company only. Today, five small grandchildren enjoy sitting at our dining table, and I still use a cloth table covering. They can't wait for the candles to be lit just before we give thanks for our meal. They love it!

Discovering what works best for you and your family will take a little experimentation. There are seasons in our lives; in each season we will find ourselves responding to hospitality in a different manner. While we make our families feel special at mealtime, let's not forget to start having company over, even when children are young.

Our children grew socially as they were included in dinner-time conversations with our guests. And they expanded spiritually as we had missionaries, pastors and even strangers dine at our table. One night they listened, fascinated, as a young man who had served a prison term told us how he had accepted Jesus while behind bars.

Children have a special place in the heart of our Lord and in our hearts as well. Why not gather them to a special place at our table?

GOOD NIGHT, LORD

Lord, thank You that You cared about mealtime. Thank You that You have told us one day we will be invited to the marriage supper of the Lamb. May we treat our family with as much courtesy and consideration as any guest we would invite—including the way we cook and prepare the meals. We thank You, Lord, that You are a guest at our table too, every time we sit down. Remind us to include others at times. Lord, in the busyness of our day, help other parents realize how important it is to take time to eat together as a family. Amen.

Notes
1. Paul A. Mickey and William Proctor, *Charisma* (March 1986), p. 75, reprinted from their book *Tough Marriage* (New York: William Morrow & Co., 1986).
2. Ibid.
3. Robert C. Morgan, *Who's Coming to Dinner?* (Nashville: Abingdon Press, 1992), p. 17.

Traditions

Yet I will rejoice in the LORD, I will joy in the God of my salvation.

HABAKKUK 3:18, *RSV*

After my husband's retirement from the Space Center, we moved to north Florida and became part of a care group which met weekly at Mike and Fran Ewing's home. A bonus was attending their New Year's Eve party each year—with 20 to 40 friends. Because the Dutch evangelist Corrie ten Boom had used the Ewings' home as her "hiding place" for many years, her family's New Year's Eve tradition became theirs (and ours).

We went around the room, taking turns to tell the highlight of our year—what God had done for us and what we wanted to thank Him for.

Just before midnight Mike opened his Bible, as Papa ten Boom had done, to read Psalm 90. When the clock struck midnight, we all hugged each other and cheered in the New Year. Somewhere down the street, firecrackers exploded. The whole world had started a new year.

Then we settled down for more Scripture reading. Just as the first words the ten Booms heard in the New Year were from Psalm 91, we listened as Mike's strong voice spoke the familiar verses:

He that dwelleth in the secret place of the most High shall abide under the shadow of the Almighty. I will say of the LORD, He is my refuge and my fortress: my God; in Him will I trust (Ps. 91:1,2, *KJV*).

Then Fran repeated Corrie's usual admonition: "Don't forget, no matter what happens in the life of a child of God, the best remains. The best is yet to be."

Through the years, many families from the Ewing care group have continued this New Year's Eve custom, no matter to what corners of the world they moved. We are just one of them. Traditions. We either love them or fear them. But we all have them. So let's consider how we can build God-honoring traditions to make ours a household of blessing. We don't have to wait until Thanksgiving, Christmas, Easter or birthdays. Family reunions, biblical feasts such as Passover or even significant family events like graduations or wedding receptions provide opportunities to begin new traditions.

GOOD NIGHT, LORD

Lord, traditions can be fun or tedious. Help us all to establish meaningful ones to mark milestones in our lives. I personally find it sobering to usher in a new year by reminiscing back on the ways You have worked in our lives. It helps me to take inventory, so I can thank You for each detail that comes to mind—of times when You intervened, protected, guided, opened doors of opportunity, brought special people into my life, spoke personally to me in a trial I was walking through. Thank You, my Lord. Amen.

Honor to Moms

Children, obey your parents in the Lord, for this is right. "Honor your father and mother"—which is the first commandment with a promise—"that it may go well with you and that you may enjoy long life on the earth."

EPHESIANS 6:1-3

I was the oldest at the luncheon table, surrounded by five young wives. The youngest was a mother of one child, a two-year-old. She was complaining because her 57-year-old mom and dad had lived with them for six weeks. She considered her parents old and set in their ways. But at her request, they had pulled up roots to move from another state to be near her. Both of them had found jobs and were soon moving into their own apartment.

"I love them," she said, "but thank heavens they're moving out and giving us our space. My mom's a better housekeeper than I am, and she can't understand why my husband and I seldom sit down to eat a meal together. Our lifestyles are poles apart. While she's a good, reliable baby-sitter, you should see—"

I quickly jumped into the conversation because her complaints were getting to me. I looked around the table and said, "I miss my mom terribly. So many days I wish I could pick up the phone and tell her something really neat about my day. Oh, how I wish I could run into her bedroom, even with her on her sickbed, and whisper something important into her ear that only a mom can understand!"

The young woman didn't respond, but the wife next to me spoke up.

"We will always miss our moms," she said. "Mine was an invalid when my children were small and they never had a normal relationship with her. Dad died before they were born. It's hard on them, not having a grandma or grandpop. How long has your mom been gone?" she asked me.

"She's been in heaven 16 years, but I'm so glad I have tape recordings of her telling stories that I can play for my family."

Soon after I got home from the luncheon, I received a phone call from a cousin out West telling me she had brought her 87-year-old crippled mom in to live with her. My aunt can't be left alone, and my cousin must assist her with everything, including baths. Every day she picks up her grandchildren at school and keeps them until their working parents come home.

I told her, "You're what's called the sandwich generation—sandwiched in between caring for a parent and grandchildren." But my cousin never complained. She was only grateful she could be there to help her ailing mother in her later years.

I thought of a framed poem one of my daughters bought me one Mother's Day and hung on my bedroom wall. I get teary-eyed every time I read this, because I'm not so sure those were always her sentiments:

For a Special Mother

For as long as I can remember
you have been there whenever
I needed a helping hand,
or just someone to talk to.
Over the years,
that has never changed.
I hope you realize if there is
ever anything I can do for you,
all you have to do is ask.
I will do my best to help.
Not to repay the things

you have done for me,
but just because I love you.

—Author unknown

Today it is my prayer that none of us—including the younger generation—lose sight of the sacrifice and devotion our parents or guardians made for us. May we truly love and honor them.

GOOD NIGHT, LORD

Lord, I am thankful for the sacrifices my mom made as a single mom to rear four children. Thank You that she was only a phone call away for all those years I was raising my young children. Thank You that she accepted me just as I was—weaknesses and all. May I be as good a role model to follow. Help younger women appreciate their moms and find ways to honor them while they are still alive. Amen.

A Lesson in Ink

Offer hospitality to one another without grumbling.

Each one should use whatever gift he has received to serve others,

faithfully administering God's grace in its various forms.

1 PETER 4:9,10

Our pastor had to leave our home Bible study early that Sunday night to catch a plane. As he rose to leave, he closed his briefcase and, in doing so, broke a bottle of black ink. It squirted across my coffee table, over my olivewood-covered Bible and onto the carpet—all the way to the entry hall. He offered his profound apologies for the accident.

"Go on and forget about it," I said. "We'll get this ink up. Really, I forgive you." I patted him on the back and ushered him out the front door.

Several men and women grabbed the towels and supplies I brought in and most of us got down on the carpet to try to remove the black spots.

I knelt beside the coffee table and began to scrub. Suddenly I laughed quietly to myself. *Here's where I knelt to give this house to You, Lord, at this very spot. So if this is Your house, this is Your carpet. And then it's Your problem, too. What are You going to do about it?*

I rubbed with the towel and cleaning solution, but the ink spots wouldn't budge. The others helping me were not getting any results either.

When I looked up and saw Lillie rocking back and forth in her chair with her eyes closed, I inwardly said a bit accusingly, *Why isn't Lillie helping, Lord?*

She's your intercessor, He reminded me.

That's right. I'd just forgotten. Lillie and her husband were several years older than the rest of us and she was indeed a prayer warrior.

After a few moments, Lillie opened her eyes and said three words that would change our evening: "Get some milk."

I ran to the refrigerator and came back with milk. As each of us scoured with a towel dipped in milk, we watched the ink spots mysteriously disappear. Lillie had an inspiration from the Lord. The carpet was clean and the only indication of that night are the black spots on my prized Bible from Israel—the one with the olivewood cover. I keep it as a reminder of that evening when God taught me a big lesson. I call it my "inkspot" Bible.

Involvement means counting the cost to follow Jesus, to allow Him to use our homes and talents. Carpets will be stained and chairs will break; but if I remember they belong to Him, it won't bother me as much.

GOOD NIGHT, LORD

Lord, it isn't always convenient to be hospitable; but while I want our home to reflect You, most of all I want my heart to be tuned to You and to those You send my way. Thank You that I can trust You to meet all my needs. Amen.

Going Home to Mother's

The LORD'S curse is on the house of the wicked,
but he blesses the home of the righteous.

PROVERBS 3:33

Over the river and through the woods to my mother's house we'll go . . . for Thanksgiving. It's the first time in more than a dozen years that most of the family will sit down together at Mother's table to eat her delicious meal of baked turkey, cornbread dressing, black-eyed peas, turnip greens, cranberry salad and yummy cinnamon rolls.

What will I say first to that freckle-faced kid brother whom I haven't laid eyes on in five years? I can tell from his pictures that the chubby kid I used to chase whenever he ran away from home has grown tall and noticeably thin. He's the one brother who could find trouble without really looking for it. The same one who beheaded all my rubber dolls when we were young, so he could have one more round, bouncy ball. The one who demanded "get lost" money from my boyfriends when I grew older.

The four of us children—now grown with children of our own—will bundle up against the wind and run along the sand beaches hugging the Gulf of Mexico to hunt for our favorite shells. Our youngest kids will pant to keep up with us. Our older ones will outdistance us. Then we'll head for the woods for a long hike. The trees will be dressed for autumn and maybe, just maybe, we'll even find one to climb.

We'll laugh and reminisce and tell our own children tales on our siblings. We may even disagree. But it will be a Thanksgiving to remember around Mother's table. And we hope it won't be so long before we're all back here again.

GOOD NIGHT, LORD

Thank You, Lord, for family. Most of all for Mother, who has tried to keep us together though we are separated by so many miles. Thank You, too, for this special holiday that has been set aside to give thanks for country, family and all our blessings. I give You thanks tonight, Lord, for blessings You have bestowed on our family in the areas of health, provision, protection, jobs, shelter, food and for this country we are privileged to live in. Amen.

His Voice Gently Speaks

He calls his own sheep by name. . . . and his sheep follow him
because they know his voice.

JOHN 10:3,4

Many times we long to know if what we are hearing is indeed God's direction. Most often, God's Spirit speaks to us in what has been called His "still small voice."

My former pastor, Peter Lord, taught us to begin to hear from God by asking Him simple questions. He suggested, "Ask God what He thinks of you. Get off alone and write down impressions you get." This is a good place to start. No doubt you will hear God tell you how much He loves and treasures you.

Pastor Lord told us the story of a young man who came to his home for a wedding reception. When the young man peered intently at the plants beside the pastor's walkway, he asked him why.

"There are 18 different kinds of crickets in these bushes," the young man replied.

Although Pastor Lord had lived in that house for years, he had never consciously heard a cricket. The visitor, however, was a graduate student in entomology at the University of Florida. He had learned to distinguish more than 200 different types of cricket calls with his natural ear in order to earn his doctorate.[1]

Oh, that we could be as familiar with the voice of God! At least 15 times Jesus said, "He that hath ears to hear, let him hear" (Matt. 11:15, *KJV*). He longs for His sheep to hear His voice and follow Him.

Once when I was staying in a hotel, I was about to take a bath when a booming voice came over the intercom: "We have an emergency. Leave the building immediately. Go to the nearest stairs. Do not use the elevators. Evacuate . . . evacuate . . . evacuate."

As I hurried down seven flights of stairs, I thought, *Sometimes I wish God's voice would boom that loud when He needs to get my attention.*

Perhaps God doesn't boom at me because then I wouldn't be required to seek Him. He wants a personal relationship based on love and trust. He respects our wills, so He chooses to let us find Him when we wholeheartedly seek Him.

The next time you have an inspired thought or someone's name pops into your head, you may soon realize it wasn't your own bright idea. You may realize it was God giving you the insight you need to solve that problem; it was God calling you to pray for someone who desperately needs direction at that moment.

We long for God to speak to us, to answer our prayers, to touch our lives and give us His guidance, protection and direction. Yet He wants even more to talk with us—not just in our little daily devotional times, but anytime, anywhere.

GOOD NIGHT, LORD

Lord, I'm so glad You care about every aspect of my life. You want to express Your love and nearness to me. You long to guide me and strengthen me for life's challenges. Forgive me for confining You to a box of my own anticipation and expectation. I give You permission to speak to me at any time and in any way. I thank You in advance that You will. Amen.

Note
1. Peter Lord, *Hearing God* (Grand Rapids, Mich.: Baker Book House, 1988), p. 27.

Company's Coming

*Therefore also we have as our ambition, whether at home
or absent, to be pleasing to Him.*

2 CORINTHIANS 5:9, NASB

It's been one of those days. Tonight I am bone weary.

Company's coming for the weekend—a huge crowd. I've got meals to plan. Stove to clean. Kitchen floor to mop. I've finished vacuuming the carpet, changing bed sheets and doing the laundry. Now I must try to sleep and not be anxious about all the work awaiting me tomorrow.

I know the blessing of hospitality will far outweigh my efforts in getting ready for our guests. Tonight I'm thinking of my friend JoAnne, whose house just shouts "Welcome" with its wonderful aromas and peaceful atmosphere. She once told me, "I spend a lot of time in prayer in my house, and it should reflect that. Whenever I expect company, I want them to feel I have prepared a place for them. Jesus has gone to prepare a place for us, so I treat my guests as He would when I prepare a place for them in my home."

Other helpful hints JoAnne gave me: It takes time to be hospitable. Be rested and dressed when company comes. Prepare as much of the meal ahead of time as possible. Do not attempt anything that is a burden—keep the menu simple. Whatever you feel good making is what you should serve.

Now as I toss and turn in my bed, I can almost hear Jesus' gentle rebuke, much like one He gave to His close friend Martha, who was distracted by all the guest preparations: "You are worried and upset about many things, but only one thing is needed. Mary has chosen what is better, and it will not be taken away from her" (Luke 10:41,42).

Yes, I too need to spend more time sitting at Jesus' feet. I need to experience His direction, His peace, His rest and love. Without His love, I'll have none to give my guests.

GOOD NIGHT, LORD

Lord, thank You for my home. Help me not be concerned about the sheer physical strength it takes to bring order out of everyday chaos. I do love this house. I leave it to Your care tonight as I fall asleep in Your peace. Let Your peace rest also on each family member as each sleeps tonight. And, oh yes, Lord, bless the friends who are coming to share our hospitality. May it be a special time for them and for us. Let me less concerned about the way things look and more concerned about how You want me to serve our guests. Amen.

Ode to a Garage

There is a time for everything, and a season for every activity under heaven: . . . a time to keep and a time to throw away.

ECCLESIASTES 3:1,6

A garage is a building for housing automobiles.

However, most garages hold everything but the family wheels. They shelter bicycles and boats. Washing machines and Dad's old coats.

Trikes, wagons and skates. Track and tunnels for electric trains.

Woodshop benches and hammers and saws. Guinea pigs, snakes and cats or dogs.

They are home for bridge tables and lawn chairs. Storm windows and portable stairs.

They hold this and that and all the other. And oh, yes, the hurricane shutters.

There are boxes and boxes of heavens knows what. Now where did we pack that machine? I have corn to pop.

There are scrapbooks and textbooks, catalogues and magazines. Pictures and postcards and most anything!

There are trunks and lamps and mops and brooms. Some yellowed newspapers and some rusty old spoons.

There are two lawnmowers, a rake and a hoe. A broken fan and a TV that won't glow.

A chair that needs upholstering and a desk that needs paint. A straw hat from Mexico and some sea shells that stink.

I know a garage that is full, full, full. *Please, nothing more,* I politely think.

Then my husband came home with 1,245 light bulbs to add. His civic club is selling; he's sure the community will buy.

In the meantime, I just sat down to cry.

GOOD NIGHT, LORD

Lord, since both my husband and I want to be better stewards of what You have given us, we do need to clear the clutter in our garage. To give or throw away, to repair or move inside. Some things are here to stay, but in a neater pile. Please help us to do this long-needed task together and without a lot of dissension. Yes, Lord, You have also shown me clutter in my heart. You are more interested in seeing me get rid of that than cleaning our garage. Please help me. I love You for showing me even my faults. Good night, Lord.

Marriage-Go-Round

However, each one of you also must love his wife as he loves himself,
and the wife must respect her husband.

EPHESIANS 5:33

Marriage counselors might not agree with me, but I have a theory about marriage. No, it won't work for every marriage, but it has for us.

When our children were young, at least once a year I took a vacation without my husband. But it wasn't a vacation from marriage.

I would drive the children all 450 miles to visit my mother, who was retired. A vacation with three children along wasn't really a vacation. Clothes still had to be washed, children disciplined and hurts soothed. But most mornings this mother slept in while grandmother played with three inquisitive children.

I found new strength from the familiar sights of the seashore and enjoyed the solitude of late walks along the sugar-white beaches. The kids and I loved fishing from Mother's boat dock, swimming in the Gulf of Mexico and going down to my brother's place to see his new horse.

Mother's home-cooked meals were just too wonderful to pass up.

When we lived near my husband's family I encouraged him to visit his family without me—at least once a year. It gave him a chance to slip back into his role of little brother for a while instead of a father with three young children clamoring and climbing all over him.

His job sent him on expense-paid trips to many locations, so he never grumbled when I felt it was time for my vacation at Mom's. One time I returned home to the most beautiful bouquet of red roses waiting on the kitchen table. Absence had strengthened our marriage bond, not weakened it.

GOOD NIGHT, LORD

Lord, now that Mother is gone, I am especially glad my husband allowed me to go visit her at least once a year. Thank You for this understanding man who knew how much it meant for me to go home. Thank You that You kept our marriage firm and that those absences—when one of us was away from the other—did not damage our marriage. We never saw those times apart as vacations from marriage! Thank You for my husband—the one You picked for me. Amen.

Out-of-the-Ordinary Days

This is the day the LORD has made; let us rejoice and be glad in it.

PSALM 118:24

It's the out-of-the-ordinary experiences that add spice to life.

It's being disgusted at 10 pesky ducks you helped to raise, who are now devouring your garden. But you still love the wild little black duck, Jo-Jo, and hope he grows up to have better manners.

It's laughing with joy at the last-day-of-school report card, especially when it's the little boy who copped so many A's.

It's being proud of your Girl Scout who got the only needle-craft badge in the troop when her mother can't even sew.

It's going to an out-of-town convention with your husband—minus the kids.

It's anxiety as you wait for the police to come and kill the sick raccoon crouched near your house.

It's letting the kids think they have you fooled—sometimes. Like the son who hides his yellow blanket under his bed each morning so he won't have to fold it neatly. Doesn't he know mothers clean sometimes? Or the 10-year-old who jumps up from the supper table to run and practice her piano. She's not really getting out of doing the dishes. They'll wait for her.

It's taking your first "trial run" at camping and discovering you brought all the wrong things.

Life is packed with unforeseen adventures. The better you bounce with the unexpected, the more fun it becomes.

GOOD NIGHT, LORD

Lord, there are days when I need to laugh more at what comes my way. Thank You for reminding me that this day, too, will pass. Yes, some of these experiences I'll hide in my memory bank, cherishing them forever. How I thank You that every day is different! Help me to savor them individually. Amen.

Career and Motherhood

Not that we are competent in ourselves to claim anything for ourselves,
but our competence comes from God.

2 CORINTHIANS 3:5

For a number of years I worked as a feature writer and photographer for the *Titusville Star Advocate*. My wonderful editor, Bob Hudson, allowed me to be home by the time my children got out of school and even gave me summers off.

Career and motherhood worked fine for me and I think my kids rather enjoyed the stories I shared with them about my exciting assignments.

Before I became a mother, I preached that nothing would ever be out of order in my house. *Before* I became a mother, that is. Then I had children. I told them we would have a place for everything. Every Saturday we put it there—on our regular pick-up, clean-up, throwaway day. But in between, our house looked lived in.

When my aunt came to visit me for the first time since I had become a mother, she was kind but she kept dropping hints about her daughter—an immaculate housekeeper and gourmet cook, the keeper of a beautiful yard and a volunteer who spent many hours each month at her children's school.

My house was clean and in reasonable order while my aunt was there, but my newspaper work assignments were a bit too much for her to believe.

One day I had to scrub up, in the same way a doctor or nurse would, to photograph a surgery at the hospital. The next day I was locked in jail with women prisoners to get a story from their

53

perspective. Another afternoon I spent 20 minutes interviewing and photographing the Apollo 13 astronauts, who were blessed to be alive after their near-fatal space journey.

My aunt smiled at my adventures and asked if I didn't want her daughter's delicious recipe for meatballs. "No," I said, thanking her just the same. I can't be a famous cook or develop a green thumb. My typing fingers itch constantly to peck out an article. And if at least once a week I can't get an exciting story, I'm terribly disappointed.

My family got as much kick as I did out of the photos I brought home of the Apollo 13 astronauts I interviewed. They thought I looked rather comical in the hospital picture showing me in a scrub nurse's mask and gown. As for being locked in jail, well that was a story they wanted to hear over and over again.

The life of a mother. Sometimes the impact of your role doesn't hit until you survey your own home as a stranger might. Then you can see that God has given you satisfying and fulfilling ways to express your unique personality and abilities.

GOOD NIGHT, LORD

Thank You, Lord, that we are all different, unique. I am so glad I don't have to fit into a mold, to be like someone I am not. Thank You that I can use my talents doing something I enjoy, and I can share them with my children. I pray they will be able to have creative jobs that excite and challenge them, just as mine have. Amen.

Letter to a First Grader

If any of you lacks wisdom, he should ask God, who gives generously to all without finding fault, and it will be given to him.

JAMES 1:5

Today you start school. Our oldest. Our first.

You are full of wonderment about what really goes on in that little red brick schoolhouse on the hill.

Well, I'll tell you, my dear. It's simple. They used to call it "reading and 'riting and 'rithmetic, taught to the tune of the hickory stick."

One of the first things you will learn in your new school is how to read for yourself. When you master that goal, my dear, the wonders of the world will unfold before you.

'Riting is most important, too. Next to talking, it's the most important means of communication. Write, write, write. Write what you feel, what you see, what you experience. Your written word will far outlive spoken words, which quickly fade.

'Rithmetic. Learn this lesson well. There will be bills to pay, budgets to set, paychecks to be stretched for food, clothing and shelter. Numbers, numbers, numbers. They will never leave you. Become their master, not their slave.

You will experience other avenues of adventure—science, art, language, music, history, literature, speech, physical education and more. As you trip through this school, sprinkle in some kindness for your fellow classmates, respect for your elders, love for God and country. Always strive to do your best.

Today we turn you over to teachers who will instruct you. We pray for them as diligently as for you that they will do their very best as they teach you.

So off to school with you now. I'll wait to cry until after you leave, so you won't see how lonely I'll be without you, even with your baby brother and sister still at home.

Mind your p's and q's.

GOOD NIGHT, LORD

Lord, today I yielded my oldest to You on her first day of school. How hard it is to let her go—to allow her to enter this new season of life. I thank You for the things You have prepared for her to experience and enjoy in her school days ahead. Help me to be the kind of encourager and helper she needs without over-mothering her. I pray for the right teachers and friends to come into her life at the right time. Guard her from the wrong companions, too. Heal the loneliness I will feel in my heart until I see her step off that school bus in the afternoon. Minister to her, too, Lord, for she must find it lonely and confusing to adjust to a new environment and schedule. Amen.

Get Out of His Way

O my son, O son of my womb, O son of my vows, do not spend your strength
on women, your vigor on those who ruin kings. Speak up for those who cannot
speak for themselves, for the rights of all who are destitute. Speak up and judge
fairly; defend the rights of the poor and needy.

PROVERBS 31:2,3,8,9

Every house needs at least one little boy. That's what I've been preaching for the past five years since one joined our household.

He has enriched our lives, broadened our experiences, challenged our patience and questioned our wisdom.

At an early age little girls begin pretending they are mothers. They have baby dolls and miniature stoves. They borrow mother's old high heels and time-worn hats. They tie frilly aprons over long skirts.

Chances are, when they are grown, they will be surrounded with real live dolls who squirm and cry and get sick. And they will have their own shiny stoves and high heels and felt hats and gingham aprons.

But take the plight of a male. He will probably settle on one occupation. It may be dull, boring, unchallenging. Or it could be exciting, promising, fulfilling.

But when he is still a little boy, he can lapse into the world of make-believe and disappear into any role that strikes his fancy.

Unlike the little girl who borrows mother's cast-off clothes, the little boy must have an array of costumes to enact his roles.

One morning he dons a cape and a fierce-looking hat that covers part of his face. He announces that for the moment he is Batman. Clear out of his way. He tries to leap from the top of his six-foot-high fort. When that fails, he ties ropes on the roof, so Batman can swing easily through the air.

Minutes later he is wearing a headdress of sweeping colored feathers and a beaded buckskin suit. He beats wildly on his leather-covered tom-tom and pauses to shoot arrows into the air. He is Indian Chief Rainwater. Out of his way!

Almost as quickly as he became an Indian chief he decides that being a cowboy would be more fun. He has a choice of a Davy Crockett coonskin cap or a genuine Western ten-gallon felt hat. Now where are those high-heeled boots? Out of his way!

But cowboy-and-Indian play grows stale. He has been inspired to become a G.I. Joe—knapsack, canteen, compass and camouflaged helmet. Out of his way! When the water and crackers give out and the little boy tires of crawling on his belly in the tall grass out behind the house, he switches costumes once more.

Now he is an astronaut. His silver-gray space suit comes equipped with two zippers and his helmet is an excellent copy of the original. He makes himself a rocket out of a tall cardboard box, but when he can't launch himself, he hollers for mother. As soon as she announces the countdown and helps him blast off, he shouts, "Out of my way!" He's off on an adventure in space that should occupy his time for at least 30 minutes.

Then Daddy comes home from work. Little boy runs for the football, protective helmet and sweatshirt with his favorite number on it. Already he fancies himself a college football player like his daddy was. He kicks the ball and runs for a 40-yard dash. A powerhouse is loose. Out of his way!

Not once has he imagined himself an engineer, a school-teacher or a salesman. His make-believe world is charged with high adventure.

One day he's bound to grow tired of swinging from ropes or beating tom-toms or bursting out of cardboard rocket ships.

But for now, at bedtime, when mother tucks in her Batman-Indian-chief-cowboy-soldier-astronaut-football star, she is also requested to cover up the fat brown teddy bear who still sleeps with him. Then they say their prayers.

GOOD NIGHT, LORD

Dear Lord, no matter what occupation my little boy chooses, help him never to forget to say his prayers. Amen.

My Hope with His Frog

A wise son brings joy to his father, but a foolish son grief to his mother.

PROVERBS 10:1

Dear First-Grade Teacher:

Rest well this summer, dear teacher. Come fall I will send to you one boy—a blue-eyed lad quite small for his age, who is already weaving big dreams.

Sometimes he says he doesn't really want to grow up, for he's heard grown-up boys often go to war. And some never come home. He loves life much too much!

He also likes chocolate ice cream, raw carrots, electric trains, guitars, animals and the boastful boy on the next block.

He hates to brush his teeth, eat cooked vegetables, put on his shoes or discard his junk.

He collects mix-matched cards, sea shells, rocks, bird feathers and records with an Hawaiian beat.

"Wait a minute" is his most-used expression. He knows his ABCs and the necessary numbers. "Why, that's kid stuff," he'll brag to his baby-sister.

He's heard tales about school principals, school-bus drivers and lunchroom proctors from the older and wiser boys who have already traveled the first-grade path. Frankly, he's a bit frightened.

He comes to you with a great deal of curiosity, a vivid imagination and an oversupply of enthusiasm.

He is presently shy but very eager to please. If you will just "wait a minute."

You will be his first link to an outside and foreign world. As you help him sort and accumulate his first scholarly facts, I trust you will do it with patience, understanding and a bit of humor. I realize he will be only one of more than 30 in your room. But you see, he's not just a number or a face to me. He's my boy, with all his faults and complexes and needs. He's my hope for the future. And whether he wants to or not, he'll grow up to be some other gal's hope, too.

Someone once said, "A boy is the hope of the future with a frog in his pocket."

I send to you, dear teacher, my hope along with his frog.

The Boy's Mother

GOOD NIGHT, LORD

Lord, I pray wisdom for my son's teacher this year. I also pray for the others who will teach him art, music and physical education. Lord, help all of them to bring out the best in my son. And may they do it with patience and understanding. Help my son adjust to his new world at school. May his first year be such a positive experience that he will always enjoy school. Lord, I pray that during his school years my child, like Daniel, will show "aptitude for every kind of learning, [be] well informed, [and] quick to understand" (Dan. 1:4). I ask in Jesus' name. Amen.

My Last First Grader

The fear of the LORD is the beginning of knowledge,
but fools despise wisdom and discipline.

PROVERBS 1:7

Dear Last First Grader:

It has become a tradition for me to write a letter as each of you begin your first grade in school.

The other day when I registered you for first grade I had to fill out a questionnaire that was a real thinkstopper. It asked how old you were when you learned to walk and talk. And if you were afraid of the dark. Or if you suck your thumb or wet the bed.

I couldn't remember without looking at the baby book when you took your first step or uttered your first "Da-da." At an average age, I am sure.

Yes, you finally stopped sucking your thumb and wetting your bed. Most kids do eventually. And yes, you've been to a zoo and to a museum—in answer to the other questions.

But that cold, white piece of paper didn't leave room to really tell all about you. Like how you caught your first fish before you were three or how many lengths of a pool you can swim.

It didn't leave room to tell about any adventures either. That you've toured 25 states in your six young years.

That you have skipped down the street in Boston where Paul Revere once rode to cry his warning. That you have climbed on the replica of the Mayflower at Plymouth Rock and have huffed and puffed up the many steps of the United States Capitol in Washington, D.C.

That you have stood at quiet attention by the gravesite of John F. Kennedy in Arlington Cemetery and watched in wonder as the eternal torch burned on. That you have waved a tiny hand at the big hand holding the torch of freedom—the Statue of Liberty in the harbor in New York.

That you have run through corn fields in Indiana and talked with Cherokee Indians in North Carolina. That you liked Mark Twain's home in Hartford, Connecticut, and were amazed at the Cyclorama reenacting the Battle of Atlanta in Georgia.

That you have seen San Antonio's Hemisfair, Arizona's deserts, Florida's caverns. Yes, you have witnessed several lift-offs of men into outer space from the Indian River some 10 miles away from the launch pad while your dad saw it from the firing room at the Space Center where he worked. Who knows, but someday you may visit the moon . . . or even Mars.

No place to record that you don't like milk or spinach, but that you love spaghetti, chocolate pudding and peanut butter on crackers. That you sometimes have an independent streak. That you hate those heavy corrective shoes you have to wear to school and much prefer to run barefoot.

So much I can't record. Especially your eagerness to read all the books you can possibly devour. My last first grader. I love you very much.

Mom

GOOD NIGHT, LORD

So much lies ahead for this child who is adventuresome and hungry to know what's on every page of a book. Lord, teach her; guide her; protect her. Give her the best teachers for her still-undeveloped talents. Give her friends who will be good influences. My last one has entered school much sooner than I was prepared for. Help me, too, Lord, to adjust to this new season of my life. Amen.

An Extra Child to Love

*All who see them will acknowledge that they are a
people the LORD has blessed.*

ISAIAH 61:9

Sometimes God sends people into our lives by divine appointment, and from then on they seem like family—at least, extended family.

One Sunday before he preached, our pastor made a startling
statement: "Jesus, the Good Samaritan needs some innkeepers."

He explained that some young people were coming to work
with our youth for a year and they needed housing. We volun-
teered to be houseparents to one of them.

While he wasn't exactly a child at 23, Mike bounced into our
lives to bring us much joy and fun. He looked like a young Abe
Lincoln with his dark beard and six-foot-three, slightly bent frame.

When he called to accept our invitation to join our family, I
phoned our pastor's wife for some advice, since she had been
foster mom to several boys Mike's age. Her guidelines to me
were helpful:

- Make him part of the family immediately by giving
  him responsibilities—like making his bed and washing his own clothes. If you wait too long, this will
  seem like punishment, not a family responsibility.
- Plan things together as a family and be sure he knows
  he's included, whether he can make it or not.
- Make time for him just as you would your own children. Let him know you love him as he is.

- Correct him in love when necessary.
- Encourage him and pray for him in all his undertakings.
- Let him be free to bring his friends to your home, for it is now his home.
- Don't be surprised if the "honeymoon" is over in three months. Remember, the real test of Christian commitment will come after this probationary period.
- He will be a blessing to you, and God will honor your obedience to love and serve Him through Mike.

Mike would roughhouse with our teenage son, Keith (with whom he shared a room), play the guitar for our morning family devotions, talk me into having 60 kids over for a youth party and leave his smelly tennis shoes perched on the dining-room table.

He was flexible, funny and uncomplaining. He lived with us for more than a year. I prayed a lot for him—especially that God would give him a wife. Robin, a gifted schoolteacher, was the answer to that prayer a year after he left us. He eventually went to seminary and became a compassionate pastor. Today they have three wonderful youngsters and Robin homeschools the oldest ones.

I'll never forget the letter Mike wrote us 10 years after he'd lived with us as our adopted son. He thanked each member of our family for what he or she had meant in his life. I cried bucketfuls as I read it.

Our enjoyable experience as surrogate parents to Mike led us later on to open our small Dallas apartment to special young people God sent our way while we—as the oldest Bible students on campus—served them food, love and counsel. And sometimes we paid their late tuition bills.

One of our favorites was Sharona, our Israel-born adopted

daughter, who at age 20 had already explored 20 countries. After she graduated from Bible school, she stayed on in Dallas to complete her degree at another college. She came over almost every weekend to eat or spend the night with us, bringing laughter, love and song into our lives.

Above our kitchen sink I kept a prayer board filled with pictures of all our "adopted kids"—some of them now serving the Lord in missions overseas. Sharona made us a Hebrew sign to hang above it: *Mishpacha*—Our Extended Family.

I still have that sign posted on my prayer board. Leah, David, Doug, Brenda, Mark, Paul, Kimmy, Jon, Daniel, Charlie, Sharona, Shannon and Beth, all smiling down on me from their photos.

GOOD NIGHT, LORD

Lord, thank You for extended family. For some people it means aunts, uncles, cousins. For us it has been the many young people You have brought into our lives and our homes. Thank You for their uniqueness and for the delight each has contributed to our family. I pray that each one of them will experience Your direction, provision, protection and extraordinary love. Amen.

A Child's Mentor

Fan into flame the gift of God, which is in you through the laying on of my hands. . . . What you heard from me, keep as the pattern of sound teaching, with faith and love in Christ Jesus. Guard the good deposit that was entrusted to you—guard it with the help of the Holy Spirit who lives in us.

2 TIMOTHY 1:6,13,14

Think about the children in your life—natural born or surrogate. Then ask yourself the question one author asked that greatly challenged me:

> What would happen if the mature men and women of your church decided to hide the children and young people of your church in their hearts for a lifetime? What if each child had a lifelong prayer supporter, a lifelong cheerleader, a lifelong partner to call before walking out on a marriage or jumping out of a window after a devastating financial loss? What difference would it make?[1]

I pondered this for some time. Then the opportunity door opened. Our church's youth pastor approached me after a service. "I'm looking for some Abrahams and Sarahs, some Hannahs and Annas, some Priscillas and Pauls and Timothys to come share with our teenagers. Will you help?"

I invited 10 strong leaders in our church to talk with the high-school youth. Our goal: to encourage them to find their individual God-given ministry gifts and talents. Each adult briefly shared what his or her gifts were—evangelism, praying for the sick, prophecy, intercession, praying for the nations, interpreting dreams or visions and others. There were moms, dads, singles and career people, all representing a variety of walks of life and spiritual gifts.

The youth then came for individual prayer from one or more of the adults. They could choose whom they wanted to pray with them, and they could go to more than one adult. I prayed for several to have their gifts of creative writing stirred up.

A week later the adults repeated this prayer session with the junior-high class.

As a follow-up, each month one or more of the adults returned to teach from their own expertise: "How to Hear God's Voice"; "How to Pray Specifically"; "How to Know If You Have Prophetic Gifts"; "What to Do with a Dream God Gives You."

The results of our hands-on ministry? We have taken those young people into our hearts—especially those who sought us out for individual prayer. They shared with us their deepest dreams and desires and asked us to stand in the prayer gap with them to see them fulfilled in God's perfect timing.

Who can say whether or not our commitment will last a lifetime? Maybe yes, maybe no. But at least it's a start.

I've been taking several of the youth on ministry trips with me to let them gain firsthand experience of praying for audiences as they sit observing and asking the Holy Spirit to teach them how to pray specifically.

While you may not have had a prayer mentor when you were a teen, it's not too late to start mentoring a spiritually ready youngster right in your own church or backyard.

GOOD NIGHT, LORD

Lord, thank You for the hunger I sense among the young people today—a hunger to know You and use their gifts for Your Kingdom purposes. Help us to connect with the ones You want us to mentor, and may we set aside the time needed to do a good job. Lord, protect our children from evil; direct them in Your paths. Give them wisdom along with their understanding. Amen.

Note
1. Bobb Biehl, *Mentoring* (Nashville: Broadman & Holman Publishers, 1996), p. 160.

What Will I Be?

For we are God's workmanship, created in Christ Jesus to do good works,
which God prepared in advance for us to do.

EPHESIANS 2:10

"What will you be when you grow up?" That question was tossed about around our dinner table tonight. What career choices will my children make? While they know what their special talents are, they aren't sure of the exact career to pursue.

At least they were thinking as they threw out such options as interior designer, librarian, writer, computer programmer, graphic artist, clothing store owner, seamstress, champion surfer.

For the son who shows talent and interest in graphic arts, I'll start to pray that God will use his gifts as He did one of the Israelites who helped build the tabernacle tent. Paraphrasing a bit, I can pray this Scripture:

> May God fill Keith "with the Spirit of God, in wisdom, in understanding and in knowledge and in all crafts-manship; to make designs" (Exod. 35:31,32, *NASB*).

For the daughter who likes to work with fabrics and with her hands, sewing clothes and making worship banners, I can pray another Scripture:

> Lord, fill my daughter Quinett "with skill to perform every work of an engraver and of a designer and of an embroiderer, in blue and in purple and in scarlet materi-al, and in fine linen, and of a weaver, as performers of every work and makers of designs" (Exod. 35:35, *NASB*).

For my daughter Sherry, who loves to read and write, I can paraphrase God's word to Jeremiah: "Write in a book all the words I have spoken to you" (Jer. 30:2).

Tonight, before I turned off the bedside light, I reread portions from a very old book. Tomorrow I'll type up some prayers from it based on Scripture so that I can make them my prayers for my children. In the name of Jesus Christ:

> I pray for the right ideas to come to my children in perfect sequence and in perfect order, and in the right time and in the right way. I pray for their actual needs to be met by the right supply in the right way and at the right time. I pray for their wills to be completely and utterly Your will. I pray that You, O Father, will open the door to the right work that will enable them to make their finest contribution to mankind. Amen.[1]

Scriptures to meditate on that relate to what God has done and will do in the lives of His children: Mark 11:24; John 5:15, 11:22, 14:13, 15:16, 16:23.

GOOD NIGHT, LORD

Lord, in Jeremiah 29:11 You tell us You have plans for us. I thank You that You know the plans You have for my children. Plans to prosper and not harm them, to give them a future and a hope. You are the One who has planted creative gifts and talents in them. Help my children to get the best training and teaching they will need to sharpen their giftings so they can eventually become financially secure. I pray they will not take a lot of detours before finding the career You have for each of them. It's my hope too, Lord, that they will make a godly contribution to mankind in their generation. May they meditate on Your Word and seek Your wisdom about all decisions they will face. Amen.

Note
1. Glenn Clark, *I Will Lift Up Mine Eyes* (New York: Harper & Brothers Publishers, 1937), p. 19.

Unconditional Love

Love must be sincere. Hate what is evil; cling to what is good.
Be devoted to one another in brotherly love.

ROMANS 12:9,10

We parents are bound to face disappointments when rearing our children. Sometimes we have such high expectations; when they don't measure up, we're disappointed, maybe even angry at them.

Could it be that our parental pride is offended? Or that we know they have the potential to do better? I've found that it helps if we

- examine our motives when we put such high demands on our children (ask God to adjust our motives);
- respond to our children with unconditional love by asking God to pour His love into our hearts by the Holy Spirit (see Rom. 5:5);
- tell our children over and over how much we love them (our love is not dependent on their behavior);
- pray for them continually and model a lifestyle of prayer (children, especially younger ones, "catch" prayer from parents who talk to God).

Suppose your children are grown and you blew it! You may feel guilty that you didn't do a better job of parenting. "If only" is a dead-end street to hopelessness. Surrender your guilt, fear and pride to the Lord. Though we can't change the past, we can trust God to help us make amends and move into the future with hope, not fear.

GOOD NIGHT, LORD

Lord, forgive me for holding a grudge against my child today. I responded angrily out of my own hurt and crushed expectations. I know this child is capable of doing better in school, finding a part-time job and keeping his room picked up. I'm sorry for the harsh words I spoke . . . for my rotten attitude against him. Lord, I did ask my child to forgive me. Now I'm asking Your forgiveness. Amen.

A Mother's Desire

Love is patient, love is kind. It does not envy, it does not boast, it is not proud.
It is not rude, it is not self-seeking, it is not easily angered, it keeps no record
of wrongs. Love does not delight in evil but rejoices with the truth. It always
protects, always trusts, always hopes, always perseveres.

1 CORINTHIANS 13:4-7

As my children grow up, I hope they will remember about our home that:

God comes first.

Their mother and daddy love each other.

Each child has both a talent and a personality of his or her own to develop to the fullest.

Health is to be treasured above wealth.

Hard work is a virtue, not a curse.

Friendship is one of the greatest gifts of life, especially those that withstand the tidal waves of years.

Sunday is the happiest day of the week, the day our family worships together and later plays together.

Praying is a natural, everyday thing, not just a "sometime" anchor to grab when life seems to be tossing you wildly about.

You must reserve time for yourself each day to be alone in quiet thoughts.

Minds are made to inquire, explore and use to the best of your ability.

Books can open fascinating doors forever, and no book on our shelves is off-base for inquiring young minds.

Camping is one of those family fun times when we can recharge physical and spiritual batteries and find a comforting sense of intimacy with God by enjoying His outdoors.

Traveling is an education in itself, and we return from each adventure more keyed up about life and the world around us.

It can be a beautiful experience to recognize and celebrate the uniqueness in other people.

Because we are human, home will never be perfect. Nor will life. Brothers and sisters often disagree. But deep down there is a common bond drawing our family together.

It's simply LOVE. I hope our children never forget that little four-letter word.

L-O-V-E.

GOOD NIGHT, LORD

Lord, this was my prayer for my children as they grew up and it's now my prayer for their children. God, I pray You will always have first place in their lives and that each of us will find ways to express love to one another. Help us, Lord, I pray. Amen.

Praying Grandparents

Believe in the Lord Jesus, and you will be saved—you and your household.

ACTS 16:31

Though my grandchildren are too young to understand the meaning of the words I speak over them, I often say to the one I'm holding at the moment, "God has a purpose for your life—a destiny for you to fulfill. I pray for God to prepare you for that destiny." If we have grandchildren nearby, we have the rare privilege of helping to nurture them in the love of the Lord.

A grandmother wrote to me about her dilemma of wanting to continue to spend time with her grandchildren and needing a paying job to help support herself and her husband after his unsuccessful job hunt. She wrote of a grandparent's ability to give deep spiritual impartation to grandchildren:

> I sense that I am in the heavenlies looking down and viewing the goings on in their lives and can see the situation as God does. He then shows me how to pray and the discernment of what is really being dealt with in the Spirit. As I considered the reality that I would no longer be able to spend that time with my grandchildren, and helping my daughter or daughter-in-law, I found myself grieving. On the other hand, I didn't want to be disobedient to a gift of a job to supply our needs.

Without any preconceived ideas, she and her husband began to pray for a miracle. On the day she was to report to her new workplace, her husband got a job. She continues to spend several hours a week teaching spiritual truths to her grandchildren.

If grandchildren don't live close, we can still pray for them and write them letters, letting them know about those prayers.

In America, families are often separated by hundreds of miles—some because of job responsibilities; others because of divorce, in-law problems, financial lack or general alienation.

One friend experienced the heartache of having her beloved grandchildren ripped away from her by divorce as their mother relocated to another state. This grandmother finally asked the Holy Spirit to take away her pain and replace it with hope. In the midst of her healing process, she realized that good-bye doesn't necessarily mean forever. So she prays constantly for them.[1]

Another friend, who seldom sees her grandson and grieves because he doesn't live in a Christian home, came up with a creative way to reach him. She and her husband put together a "treasure box" with small books of the Bible especially written for children, coloring books of biblical characters, a key chain and other small things purchased at a Christian bookstore. Whenever they visit, their grandson whips out his treasure box from under his bed and talks to them about what he's learned from the Bible. "Sometimes I go out under the big tree and read these books and I talk to God," he confided to them on their last visit.

This grandmother literally prays hours for her precious one and is assured that he will walk in the ways of the Lord. In the meantime, she keeps asking God to show her other ideas to teach him Christian principles.

GOOD NIGHT, LORD

Dear Lord, help us to be sensitive to the needs and concerns of our grandchildren, whether they live close by or far away. May we impart wisdom and encouragement to them. Help us to put forth a positive influence in their lives. We ask in our Savior's name. Amen.

Note
1. Quin Sherrer and Ruthanne Garlock, *How to Pray for Your Children* (Ventura, Calif.: Regal Books, 1998), p. 207.

Anyone Home?

In my Father's house are many rooms; if it were not so, I would have told you.
I am going there to prepare a place for you.

JOHN 14:2

I was home that Sunday morning because I'd attended Saturday-night church services. About midmorning I heard a light knock at my door and went to answer. There stood my 20-month-old grandson, Benjamin.

"Home? Home? Anyone home?" he asked, a big grin on his face.

I was startled to see him standing there. He had run away from his own home. He knew his grandmother's arms would be waiting, and he was lonesome for me.

Safe. Sound. Secure. Food, fun, hugs and cheers.

But he had crossed the street alone and it concerned me. How glad I was that I was home to hold him and get him back to his mother.

"Home? Anyone home?" God is waiting in heaven with His arms outstretched, not only for the day to bring me home but to have an intimate time each day, listening and talking with me. But it's up to me to take the time for Him.

GOOD NIGHT, LORD

Lord, thank You that You are always home. I can always talk to You. And when I think about Your eternal home I pray that You will help me influence others so they, too, will know life forevermore with You. Some have run away from You; others are just waiting for the outstretched arms of someone here on earth to love them into Your kingdom. Let me be willing hands extended—Your servant. In Jesus' name. Amen

Bless the Grands

These commandments that I give you today are to be upon your hearts.
Impress them on your children. Talk about them when you sit at home and
when you walk along the road, when you lie down and when you get up.

DEUTERONOMY 6:6,7

The visiting preacher told us how his only grandson, now 10, has always spent one or two nights a week sleeping over at Grandpoppa and Grandmama's home. After the youngster is asleep, his grandad spends a few moments standing over him, touching him lightly and praying softly a blessing of love and affirmation: "I love you. I love you. I love you unconditionally. Nothing you can ever do will cause me to cease loving you."

I smiled thinking of our own five grandchildren, ages two to five, who live near us. We delight to pray over them each time their parents bring them by.

Whenever three-year-old Benjamin walks into our house, he heads for the bookcase where the bottle of anointing oil is kept. He takes it to his Papa LeRoy to anoint him with the sign of the Cross. He stands still as his granddad prays over him, asking God's protection, provision, blessing and destiny. Three-year-old Samuel and two-year-old Victoria wait their turns to be anointed and blessed, too.

As I watch LeRoy pray over our grandchildren, I'm reminded of Jacob calling Joseph's two sons to him and blessing them before he died. Grandparents in biblical days had much influence on their grandchildren's lives. I'm sure the righteous ones constantly prayed for their grandchildren.[1]

The Hebrew people believed, too, that there was an impartation to the one anointed with oil—that it was not only a symbolic gesture but an actual impartation of endowment of the life of

God. In their book, *The Blessing,* authors Gary Smalley and John Trent say that a family blessing includes the following:

- meaningful touch
- a spoken message
- attaching "high value" to the one being blessed
- picturing a special future for the one being blessed
- an active commitment to fulfill the blessing[2]

According to Smalley and Trent, the verb "to bless" in Hebrew means to bow the knee, to show reverence or to esteem the person as valuable.[3] The dictionary defines "bless" or "blessing" as wishing a person favor, wholeness, benefit, happiness, prosperity.

How loved the children must feel to have their grandparents pray over them, bless them and impart love in a special way.

GOOD NIGHT, LORD

Lord, thank You that our grandchildren want the blessing and impartation from their granddad that comes when he anoints them with oil, lays a hand on their head and prays for them aloud. May this never be seen as a taken-for-granted ritual, but one that is sacred, cherished and very special. Pour out Your Spirit on these grandchildren, Lord, much as You did when the prophet Samuel anointed David and the Spirit of the Lord came upon him from that day forward. Amen.

Notes
1. Quin Sherrer and Ruthanne Garlock, *How to Pray for Your Children* (Ventura, Calif.: Regal Books, 1998), p. 205.
2. Gary Smalley and John Trent, Ph.D., *The Blessing* (Nashville: Thomas Nelson, 1986), p. 24.
3. Ibid., p. 26.

The Next Generation

I will utter hidden things, things from of old—what we have heard and known,
what our fathers have told us. We will not hide them from their children.

PSALM 78:2-4

Sometimes my oldest grandchild, five-year-old Kara, crawls up beside me on the couch. "Tell me about my daddy when he was small," she'll ask.

Grandparents are superqualified to do that. But I have to be selective in what I share. At her age I don't want her to know about his times of disobedience—biting his two sisters, scaring them with frogs and other reptiles or rowing a boat out in the choppy Indian River.

Instead I want to tell her all the positive episodes I remember—his gusto for camping, skateboarding, surfing, art lessons, rock collecting, even chasing armadillos. How tender his heart was toward animals. Once he even brought home a tiny owl we named "Whooty" to nurse back to health.

I'd like to tell her about the time he was playing backyard football with his friends and broke his arm. His dad and I, enjoying a rare vacation alone, had to drive 450 miles home that night to sign the papers so the doctors could operate on his arm.

He told me that the day when he turned five and started kindergarten he would tie his own shoes and make his bed. And that's exactly what he did.

I was very proud of him. As he matured he was polite and helpful, opening doors for women and the elderly, stopping to help a stranger change a flat tire. Someday, he said laughing, he would write a book called *Holding the Light* because that's what he did so much for his daddy while working under the car.

As he grew older, he was his sisters' protector. Pity the poor boys who tried to tease them!

I'm saving some exciting stories to share with Kara when she's older and can laugh along with me. Like the time when I took him with his friends to the ocean to surf and they'd neglected to tell me storm warnings were up. A hurricane was coming our way!

I don't just want her to know about her dad. I want her to know my mom too, who died a dozen years before she was born. How glad I am that I recorded some of her stories onto a cassette tape so that her great-grandchildren can enjoy her memories, too!

To make sure they don't forget, I'm leaving Kara and her younger sister, Evie, and our other three grandchildren a journal I wrote of our family history. Just as the Bible records family history and the wonders God did through families, so we pass our stories from one generation to the next.

GOOD NIGHT, LORD

Lord, thank You for the opportunity today to reach into my memory bank to tell my granddaughter some fun stories about her dad when he was young. My desire is to always choose stories that are uplifting to encourage and challenge her in her growing-up years. Lord, I'm asking for other creative ways to pass our memories from one generation to the next. Amen.

Need a Miracle?

I am the LORD, the God of all mankind. Is anything too hard for me?

JEREMIAH 32:27

"Expect great things from God; attempt great things for God." The English clergyman William Carey, considered the father of modern missions, made that his motto. My writing mentor, the late author Jamie Buckingham, passed it on to me. Both of us kept it above our computers as we wrote.

How many times I've expected little because I've forgotten that with God nothing is impossible (see Matt. 19:26).

Take Carey for example. He faced monumental challenges. In 1786 he became an ordained minister at age 25. When he expressed his burning desire to be a missionary, one superior told him bluntly, "You're an enthusiast. When God desires to converse with the heathen, He'll do it without consulting you or me." Of course, this devastated Carey.

Carey 's friends considered his ideas extravagantly imaginative, and he was branded a renegade. Everywhere he turned he faced opposition. Just as he was about to abandon his vision, he met a man who had been abroad—a man who enthusiastically encouraged him. Carey's dream was rekindled.

Finally, he knew how he could go to India: with the help of others. One day Carey sat down with some friends and held up a common rope.

"I will go down to India," he said, "if you will hold the rope." By this he meant praying for him, supporting him financially and communicating to the churches back in England regularly. They agreed to be partners in his vision.

Carey went to India. As a result, the Bible was translated into 11 languages. By late 1792, a resolution was adopted creating the first Protestant mission agency. Carey knew he could not have gone to India without his partners back in England who were "holding the rope."[1]

Sometimes God gives you a dream. You think it can't happen. It would take a miracle. Yet, many of us do not really expect great things from God. Sometimes when we get a little breakthrough we hesitate to say it was a miracle. But what if it was?

As Jamie Buckingham once wrote: "Miracles reveal the nature of God. Thus, there are no big miracles and little miracles. All miracles are big—for they reflect the nature of our big God."[2]

What household doesn't need a miracle of sorts right now? Finances. Reconciliation. Decisions and choices.

The God we serve is not a helpless, hopeless God. He's the Creator of all the universe. Nothing is too hard for Him and nothing is too hard for us to believe Him for.

GOOD NIGHT, LORD

Lord of miracles, how we need a miracle in the next few days. You know better than we do how to turn this desperate situation in our family around to bring good. Lord, tonight I put my trust and faith in You to bring something beautiful out of this mess. Lord, if I am to share our dilemma with others, show me clearly. Maybe You want them to be part of the miracle process. Not only do I expect great things from You, I trust You to help me attempt great things for You. Thank You, precious Lord. Good night.

Notes
1. John C. Maxwell, *The Power of Partnership in the Church* (Nashville: Thomas Nelson Publishers, 1999), pp. 79-81.
2. Jamie Buckingham, *Miracle Power* (Ann Arbor, Mich.: Servant Publications, 1988), p. 10.

Sour Days Turn Sweet

He has sent me [Jesus] to bind up the brokenhearted . . .
to comfort all who mourn.

ISAIAH 61:1,2

A letter from a friend today touched me deeply. She said,

> Some things are supposed to be sour—like sour cream, lemons for tea, lemon-pepper, lemonade, even lemon pie or cake, or as an ingredient in a recipe. As the purposes of God are revealed—like when Moses put the tree in the bitter waters and the waters were made sweet again—so are some seasons of our lives. I believe that season of my life is over and I am receiving sweetness from the Lord. Though the sour was a necessary ingredient, I am looking forward to these days ahead in anticipation and expectation.

GOOD NIGHT, LORD

Lord, I pray Your richest blessings on this dear friend. Only You know what heartache she has experienced—from losing her husband and a child in death, to dealing with challenges related to her other children. She's known grief, disappointments and setbacks. But I've watched her closely as she's pressed in closer, still closer to You. Your love through her has touched my life profoundly. May her years ahead be seasoned well with sweetness as only You can do. Amen.

Another Woman

So that there should be no division or discord or lack of adaptation [of the parts of the body to each other], but the members all alike should have a mutual interest in and care for one another.

1 CORINTHIANS 12:25, AMP

Jean was like a sister to me for a dozen years, standing in the prayer gap as a faithful prayer warrior—traveling with me, praying with me once a week. Truly I considered her part of my extended family.

Then she died unexpectedly—and not yet turned 50. Tonight I'm to have dinner with Jean's husband, Glenn, and the new woman in his life. Somehow I feel betrayal at having to go. My dear friend has been dead less than a year now and he may remarry soon. His new love is younger and prettier and has two young children to rear, while Jean and Glenn were already grandparents.

I'm aching inside.

GOOD NIGHT, LORD

Lord, let me see this from Your perspective. Glenn is lonesome—so alone and very inept at keeping house and cooking. He needs someone to love him—to share his bed, admire the sunsets with him, go sailing on his boat and help keep his house in order. I'm selfish to hold on to the memories of Jean so tightly, resenting someone else occupying Glenn's heart and home. Lord, bring me to a place of acceptance, so I can bless this new union. Help Glenn to be a good husband and a wise father to the children who will soon call him "Dad." Help his own son and grandchildren adjust to this new blended family. I thank You in advance. In Jesus' name. Amen.

Reaching Her Neighbors

[Jesus said,] "Love your neighbor as yourself."

MATTHEW 19:19

Grandma Lucy, the oldest resident of the trailer park, lived in a faded mobile home in a location known for its hot and humid climate.

Most would consider it an unbearable place to live, considering the roar of motorcycles, loud music, numerous verbal disputes, exhaust fumes from the nearby highway and smell of garbage in the dumpsters. The police came through regularly.

Lucy did without air-conditioning to save money. But she had a plan to touch her neighbors. Before the hot sun rose, she would get up very early in the mornings to bake cinnamon rolls. Passersby noticed the delectable fragrance. Lucy went to her door and invited them in. Certain ones came each day. She'd offer some homespun wisdom along with a hot cinnamon roll and a few words of encouragement for their day. Over time and in a natural way, she would introduce her new friends to Jesus, her Savior.[1]

A little widow living on social security in an undesirable neighborhood made a difference in the lives of numerous people who came to her door.

When I read her story I thought of many other people—probably myself included—who would have tried every way to escape from that environment. Yet Lucy, living on a limited pension, turned ordinary days into something beautiful, simply because she was an ambassador for Jesus in her own neighborhood. Loving, encouraging, offering hospitality, always thinking of others. And no doubt those new friends became her extended family.

GOOD NIGHT, LORD

Lord, thank You for the example of this giving woman who, despite her lack of material comforts, shared with others. Help me to be as interested in reaching others with the gifts You have given me. Give me resourceful ways to touch my neighbors, too. Amen.

Note
1. Kathy Deering, *Spiritual Gifts for Women* (Ann Arbor: Mich., Servant Publications, forthcoming).

A Mutual Friend

You are my friends if you do what I command. I no longer call you servants,
because a servant does not know his master's business. Instead, I have called you
friends, for everything I learned from my Father I have made known to you.

JOHN 15:14,15

As I boarded my plane in Colorado Springs, the young man ahead of me turned and smiled. *Military,* I thought to myself, observing his short precision haircut. After all, we have three military bases here.

When we got off in Chicago to make connections to other airplanes, I was surprised to find him waiting for me.

"We have a mutual friend," he said, smiling again.

"We do?" I couldn't think of anyone I knew in the military in Colorado Springs. Or how the young man whom I had never seen could know me.

"Who is it?" I asked, as we walked on down the corridor.

"It's the Jewish Carpenter from Nazareth," he said.

"Yes, I know Him. But how did you know?"

"Lady, I saw you reading your Bible on the plane."

When he learned I was running late, he grabbed my hand luggage and escorted me to my next gate. I'd barely caught my breath as I boarded the waiting plane. I didn't have time to thank my military escort—God's messenger to me for the moment—nor to tell him I have a sign in my office that reads, "My boss is a Jewish carpenter."

How many other flights have I taken when I was not such a good ambassador for the Lord? Or how many times have I stood in the checkout line at the grocery store, grumbling because of the long line, or fussed out loud in the post office when there are 20 people ahead of me?

GOOD NIGHT, LORD

Lord, wherever I am, wherever I go, help me to be conscious that others are watching me. I want to reflect Jesus. Prick my conscience when I am not modeling the character of Christ. I fail so many times, Lord. I'm sorry.

Thank You, too, for an occasional encouragement when someone recognized even in the midst of a crowd that we had a mutual friend because we both know Jesus. Amen.

Five Blessings

God our Savior . . . wants all men to be saved and to come to a knowledge of
the truth. For there is one God and one mediator between God and men, the
man Christ Jesus, who gave himself as a ransom for all men.

1 TIMOTHY 2:3-6

Could our communities be truly transformed by Christ if every
neighbor and neighborhood were prayed for daily?

God's heart desire is for all people to be saved and for all to
"live peaceful and quiet lives in all godliness and holiness"
(1 Tim. 2:2).

Christians from numerous churches in our city came
together this spring to pray for our neighborhoods. The goal
was for each person or couple to pray blessings over five neighbors and then to be available to them when needed. We agreed
to pray:

Five blessings for
Five neighbors for
Five minutes a day
Five days a week for
Five weeks

Each member of our congregation willing to participate
took a sheet of paper with this suggestion on it: Who is your
neighbor? Jesus described a neighbor as someone you meet
along life's road who needs your help. Think of the word
BLESS to remember five important ways to pray for your
neighbors.

B - Body—health, protection, strength
L - Labor—work, income, security
E - Emotions—joy, peace, hope
S - Social—love, marriage, family, friends
S - Spiritual—salvation, faith, grace[1]

Always pray with a clean heart. The prayers of the righteous are "powerful and effective" (Jas. 5:16). Pray with compassion. Be like Christ, who was moved with compassion toward the needy (Matt. 9:36). Pray with persistence (Acts 12:5; Jas. 5:17).

My husband and I pray together each morning for five families in our neighborhood who are not professing Christians. We are believing for some spiritual breakthroughs and some opportunities to bless them in practical ways.

GOOD NIGHT, LORD

Lord, I know it is not Your will that any perish and yet some of my neighbors don't know Jesus as Lord. I pray that they will turn from darkness to light, from Satan's kingdom to God's kingdom. Grant them repentance leading to the knowledge of the truth. Show me practical ways to bless them and to share the gospel's message. Amen.

Note
1. Alvin Vander Griend, *Intercessors for America Newsletter* (March 1999), p. 2. Alvin Vander Griend is director of HOPE – Houses of Prayer Everywhere. For more information contact HOPE at 1-800-217-5200.

Pass the Prayer Mantle

*We will tell the next generation the praiseworthy deeds of the LORD, his power,
and the wonders he has done . . . so the next generation would know them,
even the children yet to be born, and they in turn would tell their children.*

PSALM 78:4,6

We must pass the move of the Holy Spirit to the next generation, influencing children and grandchildren to become radical for God. Scripture clearly admonishes Christian parents to instruct their offspring in the ways of the Lord. I believe biblical evidence shows that grandparents can also help in developing their spiritual direction. I try to speak into the lives of our five preschoolers when possible, and I believe more is "caught" than just taught.

For instance, over Christmas two-year-old Samuel lost baby Jesus from our nativity scene. When Lyden Benjamin, his three-year-old cousin, came to play and discovered this, he was clearly upset. He went through our house, calling out, "Jesus, where are you? Come back to our house. Come back to our house to stay!" How I pray that three-year-olds across our nation will cry out, "Jesus, come to our house to stay!"

Over the holidays I visited a church where children crowded the altar during the singing and worship, without even an invitation to come forward. Some were praying, some weeping, some kneeling, some lying prone. I thought of something my pastor, Dutch Sheets, had said a few weeks earlier: "When you anoint the next generation and they do more than you—that's success and God is blessed."

When Jesus wanted to illustrate who was the greatest in the kingdom of heaven, He called over a little child and said, "Whoever welcomes a little child like this in my name welcomes me" (Matt. 18:5).

Scripture says that in the last days God will pour out His Spirit on all flesh and the children will prophesy (Joel 2:28). It's time to prepare these children for their destiny in God. We can do that by teaching them to talk to God when they are toddlers; by modeling a lifestyle of prayer; by giving them prayer tools—books, videos, a prayer vocabulary; by sharing our Christian values, roots and heritage verbally and in written form for them to keep.

One of our daughters has a prayer pattern with her children: As soon as she straps her toddlers into their car seats, she asks them to join her in prayer. They fold their little hands as she asks God for peace and protection on their journey. They chime in their "Amen" in unison.

Only God knows what will happen if we pray for children and leave our footprints of faith for them to follow. Let's pray that our sons and daughters, grandchildren, nieces and nephews will be salt and light to their generation—used by God to influence an ungodly world.

GOOD NIGHT, LORD

Oh, Lord, how we yearn for all our family—married and blood relatives—to know Jesus personally as Lord. Come and invade our hearts and homes. Though the three-year-old doesn't know the difference in his home and his grandparents', he knows the desperation of needing Jesus to be in our house. Help me to remember the lesson of this little voice. May I always have time for the children You send into my life. May I have a positive influence on them, and may I never forget to tell them the great things You have done. Amen.

PART TWO

Praying Through
BATTLE DAYS

I once had the privilege of interviewing a presidential hopeful for a Christian newspaper. (He later won the presidency!) My private interview with him was "watched over" by several Secret Service men as we rode in the back of a vehicle taking him from the airport. The men wore communication devices—tiny earpieces and little buttons on their lapels.

When we arrived at the place for the candidate's campaign speech, Secret Service agents watched not only his every move but carefully scrutinized everyone in that room. Even the food was tasted before he was served.

Whenever I think of the security involved for a national statesman, I think of God's still greater watchful care over us. But I'm also reminded of His call to us to be "secret service" bodyguards for the field of influence He has called us to. We are living in times of uncertainly when we must be alert and on guard—on the defensive!

We've already discussed how God put Adam in the garden to "tend and keep it"—meaning to watch over it (Gen. 2:15). God also wants us to keep the enemy out of the territory He has entrusted to us. He wants us to guard the boundaries of our garden—our bean patch—as a watchman would.

My pastor, Dutch Sheets, says, "What could have been in the garden before the Fall to guard, keep or protect from in the garden? Only the serpent."[1] Our role, he says, is to "keep the serpent out! Guard or protect that which God has entrusted to our care from the subtle encroachment of the serpent. Keep him out of your garden! . . . Your home, family, church, city, nation! . . . Keep him out!"[2]

As guardians, we go to our prayer closets and invite the Holy Spirit to show us how to pray; we also set boundaries to keep the enemy out.

A friend of mine in Nebraska told me that one spring, she and her two daughters and a daughter-in-law prayed over their husbands' farmlands every day as they walked the land. Their husbands had shown them the boundary lines to walk as they prayed. Most days they walked two miles. But on some days they covered six miles, going from fence post to fence post. The women prayed for protection from insects, crop diseases, hail and drought. They asked God to give their husbands wisdom to farm and market the crops. They prayed for angels to be assigned to the fields.

"We saw amazing results," she told me. "It was one of our better years. Some farms felt the bankruptcy pressure really hard that year. While our husbands made prudent decisions, other farmers made unwise marketing decisions. Our crops made a profit and we saw no storm or insect damage."[3]

What she and her family were doing was watching over, or tending, their fields—their literal crops—in the spiritual realm.

We are called to do the same as we watch and pray over our fields, which consist of those people within our realm of influence—our family members, coworkers, friends, neighbors, community. Your realm of influence may be even broader.

INTERNAL FOES

It's a bit easier to recognize some of the external forces we need to guard against, but some of the less obvious threats to our bean patch involve the burdens we carry around without fully realizing how they are weighing us down. These include inner attitudes and emotions that can be destructive to our well-being and keep us from enjoying close fellowship with the Lord.

I once heard a pastor say that God wants to do something *in* us before He can do something *through* us. I have discovered that the "do something" is to remove obstacles that keep me from walking more closely with the Lord. I need to cast off the "dead weight" I carry around.

Maybe you, like me, are sometimes so burdened with cares that you feel hardly able to stand. Perhaps you are coping with depression or anger because of injustices piled on you at home or work. Or you're experiencing prolonged grief over the loss of someone or something. Or you have a severe addiction that's affecting your health and your pocketbook.

Maybe guilt badgers you because your children are on drugs or your husband is threatening to leave.

Your burden is just too heavy.

If that's the case, maybe you can identify with the woman in the Bible who walked bent over for 18 years with her face toward the floor. She was unable to stand straight or do much of anything for herself. One day she met Jesus in the synagogue. He noticed her plight and reached out to her with words of liberation: "Woman you are loosed from your infirmity" (Luke 13: 12,13, *NKJV*). Then He laid hands on her and immediately she was made straight. Her first response was to glorify God.

In essence, Jesus was saying, "Woman you are free. Lift up your head. No more bondage." Can you imagine what it was like to stand up straight for the first time in 18 years and then to gaze into the Master's eyes and see pools of love and compassion? Her burden was caused by a spirit of infirmity.

The Greek word for "loose" in this passage means "to loose anything tied or fastened; to set free, to discharge from prison; to free from bondage or disease (one held by Satan) by restoration to health."[4] Here are some burdens we tend to hold on to that Jesus longs to lift from us and replace with their weightless opposite:

- replace fear, worry and anxiety with trust
- replace grief with joy
- replace disappointment or depression with hope
- replace anger with God's peace

- replace addiction with His love and acceptance
- replace occult or cult involvement with the truth about Jesus and His blood shed for our salvation and eternal life

Often we are in bondage because we hold on to old sin patterns or habits that are diabolically opposed to God's Word. God wants us to let go of them and allow Him to work a miracle of freeing us from them.

As long as we live on this earth we will have conflict—with an invisible enemy and his evil agents in the spiritual realm, with our own inclination to sin and with a fallen world. We cannot avoid the battle days, but we can persevere in prayer and trust in God to sort it all out. These are the days He wants to do something in you before He can do something through you.

Notes
1. Dutch Sheets, *Intercessory Prayer* (Ventura, Calif.: Regal Books, 1996), p. 244.
2. Ibid., p. 245.
3. From *How to Pray for Your Family and Friends,* © 1990 by Quin Sherrer and Ruthanne Garlock. Published by Servant Publications, Ann Arbor, Michigan, pp. 152, 153. Used with permission.
4. Joseph Henry Thayer, *A Greek-English Lexicon of the New Testament* (Grand Rapids, Mich.: Baker Book House, 1977), p. 384.

Remember Roses

And if I [Jesus] go and prepare a place for you, I will come back and take you to be with me that you also may be where I am.

JOHN 14:3

Whenever I think I just can't take any more hard times—that I've reached my limit—I remember a lesson I learned from my grandson, Lyden Benjamin, when he was two.

While walking with him from my house to his, it seemed we would never get to his front door because he stopped to smell the roses all along the way. In my impatience I wanted to get on with the journey, to reach our destination. But his pleasure at the beauty and fragrance of the flowers made his walk a delight.

Suddenly I realized how I tend to hurry through life, not savoring my "golden moments" and the beauty of God's creation along the way. Yes, tough times come. But even when our paths lead through suffering, we can find flowers along the way. And with the thorns of the rose also comes the perfume.[1]

GOOD NIGHT, LORD

Lord, how glad I am that this earth is not my final home. Because of Jesus' death and resurrection I have the promise of eternal life with Him. Help me through the tough times. But don't let me forget to enjoy the perfume and beauty of each precious day along the way. Amen.

Note
1. From *A Woman's Guide to Getting Through Tough Times,* © 1998 by Quin Sherrer and Ruthanne Garlock. Published by Servant Publications, Ann Arbor, Michigan, p. 228. Used with permission.

Boundaries and Balance

I can do everything through him who gives me strength.

PHILIPPIANS 4:13

We women sometimes have difficulty maintaining a balance between helping out when there's a real need and allowing others—often family members—to lean so heavily on us that we get in an overload mode. Knowing when to say yes and when to say no is often difficult.

Sometimes we feel pressured by excessive requests and unrealistic expectations, which can drive us to frustration. By the time we do all the necessary mommy things—pack lunches, make costumes, drive the carpool, clean and cook, volunteer at school and church—we're too worn out to be pleasant at home. In fact, some women believe they cheat their families because of their own exhaustion and discouragement.

Most solutions don't come easily. But they are worth working on. For starters, ask God to show you priorities at this particular time in your life, and write down the answers He gives you.

Ask yourself: What positive step can I take at this time that would lighten my work load or make me a better, happier, more compatible woman (wife, mother, career person)?

Maybe it's saying no to the Girl Scout troop this year or buying cookies instead of baking them for the first-grade class. It may mean giving yourself one night a week away from home with a friend, just to laugh and do "girl things." Or enjoying a hot bath with no kids around—for one whole hour! Or spending a quiet evening out with your husband. Or taking no work home from the office. The main thing is to decide that you don't want to be a grouch and you will take at least one positive step toward the liberty that comes with a balanced life.

GOOD NIGHT, LORD

Lord, help me to set boundaries for my own sanity and physical well-being. I can't be all things to all people, but with Your help I can be the best person You designed me to be for this season. Help me not to resent the restrictions I work under, but to be content, knowing that I'm pleasing You and doing the best I can. Strengthen, enable, comfort and direct me, O Lord, my helper. Amen.

Avoiding Pitfalls

I know that after I leave, savage wolves will come in among you and will not
spare the flock. Even from your own number men will arise and distort the
truth in order to draw away disciples after them. So be on your guard!

ACTS 20:29-31

If our walk with the Lord is a journey, we would be wise to learn
in advance about possible pitfalls along the way. The New
Testament contains countless warnings against deception, pride,
greed, unforgiveness, wrong motives, selfishness, disobedience
and many other traps to avoid.

Each one of us is susceptible to falling into these "pits."
Scripture tells us, "If you think you are standing firm, be careful
that you don't fall" (1 Cor. 10:12). When we remain open to the
Holy Spirit, He is faithful to warn us against the traps lurking
along our path.

Here is a partial list of pitfalls to guard against. I've found that
meditating upon the Scriptures provided below helps me to recognize what I've already fallen into and serves as a warning of possible
traps ahead that may tempt me if I succumb to the enemy's schemes.

- Unforgiveness (2 Cor. 2:10,11; Mark 11:25)
- Deception (Matt. 24:4,5,11,24-26; 2 Cor. 11:3,14)
- Manipulation (2 Cor. 4:2)
- Praying soulish prayer (Jas. 4:1-3)
- Holding grudges (Eph. 4:26-32)
- Presumption (Acts 5:1-11)
- Missing God's timing (Acts 16:6-15)
- Unbelief (Heb. 3:12—4:2)
- Personal ambition; not making room for others' gifts
  (Phil. 2:3,4)

- An untamed tongue (Jas. 1:26; 3:9,10)
- Not obeying the word God gives you (Luke 6:46-49)
- Gossip; taking up someone else's offense (2 Cor. 12:20)
- Operating out of the intellect only—not being open to the Spirit of God (1 Cor. 2:12-14)
- Spiritual pride (1 Cor. 4:18-20)
- Dabbling in New Age or other godless philosophies (Col. 2:6-8; 2 Tim. 4:3-4)

Deception is a "biggie" pitfall. We are told to "test the spirits" (1 John 4:1) as we ask the Holy Spirit for discernment. Deception comes in many forms: believing teachings that are contrary to Scripture, listening to voices other than the Holy Spirit's, mixing truth with error. A book, film or teaching may sound good, but we must ask ourselves if it lines up with biblical truth. If it doesn't, we are to leave it alone.

Praying soulish prayers is asking for what we want or what we think is best, rather than praying Spirit-led prayers.

How can we avoid such pitfalls? Every day we can ask God for His wisdom. Then when we meditate on His Word, we are less likely to fall prey to deception. Listening to wholesome tapes and worship music—even Bible reading on tapes—helps us to walk in His ways.[1]

None of us set out deliberately to fall into the traps the enemy has laid for us. But little by little we can be pulled into them if we aren't alert and keeping our spiritual ears tuned to the voice of God's Spirit.

GOOD NIGHT, LORD

Lord, show me areas of my life where I may be walking in deception, presumption, unforgiveness or manipulation or in any unwholesome way that is displeasing to You. Whatever the vulnerable area is, Lord, I want to be open and humble before You. I give the Holy Spirit permission to correct me and help me to avoid these traps and to keep my feet on the path that follows Your footsteps. I ask this in Jesus' name. Amen.

Note

1. From *A Woman's Guide to Spirit-Filled Living,* © 1996 by Quin Sherrer and Ruthanne Garlock. Published by Servant Publications, Ann Arbor, Michigan, pp. 203, 204. Used with permission.

Saying No to Addictions

No temptation has overtaken you except such as is common to man; but God is faithful, who will not allow you to be tempted beyond what you are able, but with the temptation will also make the way of escape, that you may be able to bear it.

1 CORINTHIANS 10:13, NKJV

Addictions? "Not hardly!" you say. But did you know that whatever thing or activity controls our thoughts and actions—what we worship, so to speak—can easily become our bondage?

We are familiar with some obvious addictions—food, alcohol, drugs, sex. But what about addictions to shopping, work, reading romance novels, exercising and even "religious" activities?

What about those of us who collect things compulsively? One woman I know never misses a Saturday-morning garage sale or antique auction. Another woman must have that porcelain angel to add to her huge collection, even though she can't afford it.

No Christian woman would want to admit it, but if her hobby or collection or activity has that strong a grip on her life, she has made it an idol as surely as the children of Israel made a golden calf to worship in the wilderness. It's spiritual idolatry, plain and simple.

Why do we get started with an addiction? For a variety of reasons: an attempt to escape worry and anxiety; a means of reducing guilt feelings; an effort to avoid pain, confusion, failure or imperfection; an urge that says, *I must have it. I must. I can't do without it.*

Addictive behavior is only a symptom, a coping device we use to mask the pain of a deeper problem. We need to ask ourselves why we do what we do.

One woman who was caught in the trap of excessive daily exercise asked herself, *Why am I so driven to do this? Is it for compliments? For self-satisfaction? For health's sake?* In time she was able to acknowledge her imperfections and self-hatred and begin to accept herself. As a result of her self-examination, and with a lot of help from the Lord, she even cut down the number of hours she pushed herself to exercise each day.

Sometimes compulsive behavior stems from unresolved issues in our lives. Often, a professional counselor can help us uncover these issues. But a key to walking free is to depend on the Lord to help us and then to be accountable to someone who can encourage us, pray with us and correct us when necessary.[1]

A recovered drug addict said it well: "I've learned that the thing I depend upon in my life controls my life; therefore, I must depend on Jesus Christ."

GOOD NIGHT, LORD

Lord, only You can give me the strength I need to overcome the monster that grips me in my weakest area. I acknowledge that my addiction is displeasing to You and a snare in my Christian walk. I confess that I've enjoyed it and have been unwilling to give it up, but I truly desire to overcome it. I don't want to be a slave to it any longer. Help me to find someone who will stand with me in the area of accountability as I attempt, with Your help, to master it. If I need professional counseling, give me wisdom to find the right counselor. Help me, Lord, I ask in Jesus' name. Amen.

Note

1. From *A Woman's Guide to Breaking Bondages*, © 1994 by Quin Sherrer and Ruthanne Garlock. Published by Servant Publications, Ann Arbor, Michigan, pp. 130-143. Used with permission.

Dealing with Low Self-Esteem

Don't you know that when you offer yourselves to someone to obey him as slaves, you are slaves to the one whom you obey—whether you are slaves to sin, which leads to death, or to obedience, which leads to righteousness?

ROMANS 6:16

If you have ever suffered from rejection, low self-esteem, abandonment, depression or unforgiveness, perhaps you can identify with my nurse friend, whom I'll call Doris.

Doris hated Christmas. For 17 years she had put on a front, barely making it through the gift-buying and festivities with family and friends. Melancholy chased her for six weeks every holiday season. Christmas might mean joy for others but not for her. Bah, humbug!

Finally, she recognized the underlying reason: She was in bondage to past memories. Don and Doris had been married only three years when over Christmas he told her he was leaving her for a coworker. He'd asked her not to tell her parents this was their last Christmas together as a married couple.

Shortly afterward, Doris became a Christian and realized she needed to forgive her husband for his unfaithfulness and for the divorce that followed. As best she knew how, she told God that she forgave Don. But 17 Christmas seasons rolled by, filled with pain and dread—each one reminding her of her failed marriage.

One holiday she said, "Devil, you aren't robbing me of any more Christmases." She arranged a face-to-face meeting with her ex-husband in a hospital waiting room. She had gone back home to care for her ailing father. Her talk with her ex-husband brought closure to the relationship and she was able to go on with her life, her self-esteem intact.

Doris told me, "I had been in emotional bondage to him all those years. The issue was abandonment. I couldn't put the marriage back together, but I could now look forward instead of dwelling on the past. The key was choosing to really extend forgiveness and not allowing the devil to rob me of any more holiday seasons."

How do we know Doris has won her battle? She can now listen to Christmas music over the radio. And she stops at the Salvation Army kettle to drop in a contribution—painful things she used to avoid.

Doris's experience helps us understand how the enemy, Satan, can take advantage of our hurts, disappointments and insecurities to keep us in bondage.

Notice the steps Doris took to achieve victory:

1. She moved from denial to admitting she needed to address her problem.
2. She identified her former husband's abandonment as the source of her pain.
3. She took action. Though she thought she had forgiven him in a general way, healing came when she truly forgave him for abandoning her. Talking to him in person helped to accelerate her healing because he was forgiving and asked forgiveness in return (which is not always the case when we offer forgiveness).
4. Once the issue was behind her, she determined to look at Christmas with a positive attitude, no longer allowing the enemy to steal her joy.

We, like Doris, have a responsibility. We don't earn our freedom by good behavior; we must be willing to throw out the excess baggage that invites bondage. When we ask God to help us, He joins His power with our will to be liberated.

God is our loving Abba [Daddy] Father, who truly wants His best for His daughters. He longs to free us from these sins and weaknesses, and He wants us to move on with Him in joy, unencumbered by chains of bondages.[1]

GOOD NIGHT, LORD

Lord, I acknowledge that my walk with You is not all it should be. I give in to little defeats and allow the enemy to keep me in bondages of rejection or low self-esteem and, yes, even unforgiveness. I truly want You to spotlight hindrances, habits and bondages I cling to that keep me from the freedom You desire for me. Help me, Lord, I pray, in Jesus' name. Amen.

Note
1. From *A Woman's Guide to Breaking Bondages,* © 1994 by Quin Sherrer and Ruthanne Garlock. Published by Servant Publications, Ann Arbor, Michigan, pp. 20-23. Used with permission.

Fear Versus Faith

For you did not receive a spirit that makes you a slave again to fear, but you received the Spirit of sonship. And by him we cry, "Abba, Father."

ROMANS 8:15

Countless women battle private fears. "Fear" comes from a word that means sudden calamity or danger.

Some of our most prevalent fears are about abandonment, failure, disapproval, ridicule, financial lack, violence, disease, pain, death, losing a loved one, losing a relationship, losing independence, fear of the future.

It's interesting to realize that fear and faith start out alike. Both believe that something is going to happen. The difference is that fear believes something bad will happen; faith believes something good will happen.

Scripture says, "For God has not given us a spirit of fear, but of power and of love and of a sound mind" (2 Tim. 1:7, *NKJV*). The word for "power" here means strength, or ability; "sound mind" denotes good judgment, disciplined thought patterns, the ability to understand and make right decisions. So God gives us the power, or strength, to make good decisions not based on fear.[1]

The virtuous woman described in Proverbs 31 had no fear of the future, only a reverential fear of the Lord. She was praised at the city gates as a noble woman. The description of her character inspires me.

I once read an article based on a survey of 4,000 worriers. It revealed that only 8 percent of our worries are "worth the worry," and most of the things we worry about never happen. In fact, "what we worry about today we often laugh about tomorrow. Our worry is evidence of inner insecurity. As Christians, we know where to find security. . . . Take your burden to the Lord and leave it there."[2]

Over and over in Matthew 6, Jesus told us not to worry, not to be anxious, as a reminder that our heavenly Father's watchful eye is on us. He then advised, "But seek first his kingdom and his righteousness, and all these things will be given to you as well" (Matt. 6:33).

Sometimes, walking free of fear is a process; it takes time to discipline our thought patterns and walk in trust. But God provides us the power to do that if we will ask Him.

GOOD NIGHT, LORD

Lord, how I need to trust in You to work out my circumstances according to what You know is best for me. I want to give You my fear and anxiety. At the same time, I've held on to them so long that I find it hard not to live this way. Help me to move into that place of total abandonment to You, with a reverential fear that makes me appreciate Your awesomeness as well as the fact that You are my "Daddy-Father" and You know what's best. Amen.

Notes
1. *The Spirit-Filled Life Bible, NKJV* (Nashville, Tenn.: Thomas Nelson Publishers, 1991), p. 1853, referring to *Strong's Exhaustive Concordance,* #1411, #4995.
2. Fred Smith, "Wait to Worry," *The Christian Reader* (June 1993), pp. 53, 56.

Keep an Eye on the Ark

And the priests came up out of the river carrying the ark of the covenant of the LORD. No sooner had they set their feet on the dry ground than the waters of the Jordan returned to their place and ran at flood stage as before. . . . [God] did this so that all the peoples of the earth might know that the hand of the LORD is powerful and so that you might always fear the LORD your God.

JOSHUA 4:18, 24

The book of Joshua gives us insight about how to fight our personal battles—by keeping our eyes on the ark, God's presence.

After many years of slavery in Egypt and 40 years in the desert, the Israelites were finally going to enter the land promised to Abraham some 400 years earlier.

The tribes of Israel were camped on the east side of the Jordan River. God commanded them to move forward, pass over and then He would give them the battle plan to conquer the land. While He was giving them the Promised Land, they had to possess their inheritance—what was legally promised to an heir. They had to fight for it.

God encouraged them to be strong and courageous, promising to be with them wherever they went. First they needed to consecrate themselves—make themselves holy unto the Lord.

The river at this time was impassable. But God had a supernatural plan:

> When you see the ark of the covenant of the LORD your God, and the priests, who are Levites, carrying it, you are to move out from your positions and follow it. Then you

will know which way to go, since you have never been this way before (Josh. 3:3,4).

The priests who were carrying the Ark of the Covenant went and stood in the river; as they proceeded, the water from upstream stopped flowing and piled up in a heap a distance away. The priests stood on dry ground in the middle of the Jordan while all Israel passed by until the whole nation had crossed over (see Josh. 3:14-17). They took 12 stones from the riverbed and placed them on the banks as a memorial, so they could later tell their children that Israel crossed the Jordan on dry ground.

Their first battle was Jericho—and we all know that carrying the ark of the Lord was the key as they marched around the city, obeying God's specific orders. The walls fell and they took the city. But whenever the Israelites failed to obey God, they got into trouble. They learned obedience to Him during their almost 10 years of conquest.

How does this apply to you and me today?

- We believe God for a supernatural way out when the task looks impossible.
- We keep consecrated before the Lord by daily communication with Him, including time spent alone in solitude.
- We let the peace of God sustain us; when we're not walking in peace, we can't hear God.
- We remember that God always planned to give His people victory. (We can pray, "Cause me to win by going Your way, Lord.")
- We recall the things God has done for us in the past—the equivalent of building the rock memorial the Israelites set up on the banks of the Jordan.

- We leave the outcome in God's hands. We will not be aware of God's total plan and purposes until later.
- We try to obey God's instructions whether we want to or not.
- We keep our focus on the Lord, not on the problem. (The Ark of the Covenant went before the Israelites in battle, reminding them to keep their eyes on His presence.)[1]

God has a plan for us that far outdistances what we can think up. We can thank Him ahead of time for winning our battles for us.

GOOD NIGHT, LORD

Lord, thank You for biblical examples that show us Your faithfulness and trustworthiness. Help me to keep my eyes on You, my ears open and my flesh willing to do what You ask, regardless of what I think. Amen.

Note
1. Some insights for this were gleaned from a sermon by Pastor Dutch Sheets, Springs Harvest Fellowship, Colorado Springs, Colo., June 20, 1999.

God's Timing

God did not give us a spirit of timidity, but a spirit of power, of love and of self-discipline. So do not be ashamed to testify about our Lord . . . who has saved us and called us to a holy life—not because of anything we have done but because of his own purpose and grace.

2 TIMOTHY 1:7-9

Sometimes we are reluctant to do what God is leading us to do, or we run ahead of the Holy Spirit instead of moving at His direction. Either way we miss His timing.

A prayer partner, Dee Eastman, helped me to understand God's timing more clearly. She talked about God moving in seasons. Of course, the winter seasons of our life are the hardest.

One day she told me, "God may be setting us aside for a period of learning from the Holy Spirit. It is preparation for the spring. If we don't have the winter of dormancy, we won't be prepared for springtime with its blue skies, bursting blossoms, new life and fresh breezes."

I was in the midst of a long "winter season" in my life. Dee and I met together for prayer on Tuesday mornings, and we read and meditated on these verses:

See! The winter is past; the rains are over and gone. Flowers appear on the earth; the season of singing has come, the cooing of doves is heard in our land. The fig tree forms its early fruit; the blossoming vines spread their fragrance. Arise, come" (Song of Songs, 2:11-13).

Dee kept praying for springtime to come for me, and indeed it finally did. I just had to wait for God's timing.

One day I missed His timing in something that was seemingly pretty silly and insignificant. I did not ask the Holy Spirit if I was to accept the invitation to meet some friends for lunch—Christian women who loved the Lord and got together only occasionally outside their church commitments.

The night before, I had arrived home from a dynamic conference and was on a spiritual high. As soon as we'd ordered our meals, I asked the question a speaker had asked us at the conference: "What would you do if you knew Jesus was coming tomorrow?"

Silence fell! No one spoke. Then one woman replied rather flippantly, "Well, I'd still be eating lunch at the Upper Crust Restaurant."

I almost choked. As soon as I finished my meal I excused myself to get off and talk to the Lord about this. He showed me that (1) I hadn't asked Him if I should have gone to the luncheon; (2) I was in a reflective mood while they were in a fun mood, neither of which was wrong; (3) I had not settled in my own heart what I would want to be doing if I knew Jesus was coming tomorrow, and I was looking to these women to provide me some answers.

I was the one at fault, not them. They had graciously included me in their lunch plans, but I hadn't particularly "fit in." I determined next time to ask the Lord first and then not put any burdensome expectations on my friends.

We must be willing to wait for God's voice. On the other hand, when God tells us to do something, we must not delay our response and miss His timing and His best for that season of our life.

GOOD NIGHT, LORD

Thank You, Lord, for the various seasons of our lives and for friends who help us walk through them. I'm sorry I didn't listen for Your direction when I was in a winter time in my life . . . or even when I didn't ask before I accepted a luncheon invitation. How often I miss Your timing, simply because I move ahead with my plans, my wants. I'm sorry. Help me to do a better job of listening. I don't want to miss Your timing for any phase of my life. Amen.

Life's Rhythm with Balance

Repent, then, and turn to God, so that your sins may be wiped out, that times of refreshing may come from the Lord.

ACTS 3:19

In his excellent book *The Rhythm of Life*, Richard Exley encourages Christians to put life's priorities in proper perspective in four areas: work, rest, worship and play:

> How can we expect to be happy when we violate almost every principle of the abundant life? We work too long, play too fast, laugh too loud and worship too little. . . . Our only hope is to learn to love God and people instead of things.[1]

He says that so often "we are programmed for exhaustion. We are overcommitted, overextended and overworked. Rest and renewal have been replaced with busyness."[2]

The Spirit-led Christian woman will find time for rest, worship and play along with her work. She will learn to acknowledge when her body needs rest or play. And she will begin to include worshiping our Lord every day of her life.

Some good questions to ask yourself (and I'm asking them too):

- What are my priorities for right now?
- What are my God-given dreams or visions? Can I state them in a sentence or paragraph?

- Am I doing anything right now that the Lord wants me to give up? How can I put that into practice soon?
- How can I find more time for worship and study of God's Word? (Make a commitment of time allotment on a regular basis.)

Two things we can start putting into practice as we answer these questions: First, as we purpose to hear and obey God's voice, we invite Him to reveal Himself to us in a more intimate way through the Holy Spirit. Second, we do not succumb to false guilt if we don't achieve our goals based on an unrealistic timetable.

GOOD NIGHT, LORD

Lord, I admit I overextend myself. I find it hard to say no to things that I know are outside my expertise. Why do I do that? To please people, rather than You? Help me to find balance—the right rhythm to life. I want to hear You say to me tonight—not just when I've finished my race—"Well done, good and faithful servant" (Matt. 25:21). Help me to be a good steward of the talents You've given me. Help me not to overwork my physical body so that it wears out ahead of Your timing. I ask this in Jesus' name. Amen.

Notes
1. Richard Exley, *The Rhythm of Life* (Tulsa, Okla.: Harrison House, 1987), p. 108.
2. Ibid., p. 77.

Be Prepared

I will instruct you and teach you in the way you should go;
I will counsel you and watch over you.

PSALM 32:8

I've discovered I can't yet say with the apostle Paul that I'm content in whatever circumstance I find myself.

One day we got trapped in a summer cabin in a freak snowstorm that hit the Sun Belt of Texas. Sitting on the couch and wrapped in blankets, I asked my husband what lessons he had learned during this time.

He replied, "Be prepared spiritually, physically and mentally for any circumstance."

Now that's a tall order! We had run into the cabin the night before to escape the sleet. I hadn't thought to snatch my briefcase containing my Bible, notebook and manuscript I was revising. I felt almost bankrupt spiritually (though I did have a New Testament in my purse).

The car doors were frozen closed and we had no tools to pry them open. We would have to wait for them to thaw. For meals we had cheese and crackers. One person in our group, who was not wearing proper winter gear, hiked in 13 inches of snow to a tiny store for a loaf of whole-wheat bread and milk. Truthfully, I was more concerned about keeping warm than eating. To occupy our time we listened to our one Scripture chorus tape over and over, played with the two games we found in the cabin and turned the radio on and off all day. After a while boredom set in.

One of the hardest things for me was being cooped up for almost three days with a stranger who was not spiritually likeminded. In fact, our Christianity offended him. I kept playing the "if only" game. If only I had grabbed the spiritual tapes and books, the warm wool blankets and bits of food in the car before we'd run into the cabin.

I thought of Corrie ten Boom, who kept an emergency bag packed with vitamins and personal necessities in case the Nazis came to arrest her for hiding Jews. When they did come, she left the bag rather than take the chance of exposing the hiding place behind her bedroom wall. But Corrie had the most important thing: She had the Word of God hidden in her heart and she won many to the Lord while in prison.

It was two and a half days before we could dig our car out and be on the road again. On the way home I was overcome with regret, remorse and repentance for letting the Lord down because of my own unpreparedness, my unwise use of time and my failure to properly witness to the one who needed Jesus while camping there with us.

GOOD NIGHT, LORD

Lord, I'm taking another look at my lifestyle. I purpose to be better prepared for whatever circumstance comes my way in the days ahead. Thank You that You have already forgiven me, as I requested, for the mistakes I made during that storm. Now I want to be stronger spiritually for the storms that lie ahead. And I don't want to miss an opportunity to share about Jesus—even with a stranger. Help me, Lord. Amen.

Sin Always Affects Others

And when you stand praying, if you hold anything against anyone, forgive him, so that your father in heaven may forgive you your sins.

MARK 11:25

The early morning plane from Colorado to Dallas was packed with passengers—most of them dressed in business suits, which indicated they had appointments in various cities. A heavy snow was falling although it was late March. Airline personnel were busy deicing our plane.

Just when we were ready to take off, a woman sitting in front of me called a flight attendant over. I heard part of her conversation. "Check to see if a man named Craig _____ is on board. I put his luggage on for him. I didn't really know him. I don't think he boarded."

When it was certain the passenger wasn't seated, she was asked to step off the plane for further questioning. The rest of us fidgeted in our seats while the luggage compartment was searched. The moments ticked away. Thirty minutes. Forty minutes. Sixty minutes.

Nowadays, everyone is questioned initially when they check in at the ticket counter. "Did you pack this luggage yourself? Has it been in your possession the whole time?" The woman had outright lied when asked this.

Finally, she came back on board and returned to her seat amid a few angry "boos" from nearby passengers. Now we waited again—for the plane to be deiced once more.

When we reached Dallas, everyone it seemed had missed plane connections. Buses were waiting to take some of us to other terminals, even changing us to other airlines. A woman near me with two small babies began to cry. She wasn't prepared to have to get them on and off a bus and run for another plane at a different terminal. Businessmen were cursing because they'd missed their flights.

Not only did I miss my flight there, but when I got to Atlanta I was also too late for that connection. Everyone's day it seemed had been interrupted because of one woman's wrong choice—her decision to accept luggage from a stranger.

Yes, I was glad she finally came clean and admitted her mistake, and the questionable luggage was removed. It could have contained an explosive. Yet I also saw how many people's lives can be affected by one person's decision to do the wrong thing.

GOOD NIGHT, LORD

Lord, how easy it is to point my finger at this woman's bad decision. I was so angry at her because I arrived late for my appointment. She did such a silly thing, without regard for others. But You have shown me how often my own sin hurts others, too. Harsh words, a curt attitude, unwillingness to listen. Lord, I want to live more like You so that I won't damage others by my wrongdoing. Forgive me for the times when my bad choices—my deliberate sin—have wounded others. I am truly sorry. I even choose to forgive that woman, because I don't want my own prayers to be hindered, and I won't be in bondage to a chain of unforgiveness. Amen.

Our Military Personnel

You are not a God who takes pleasure in evil; with you the wicked cannot dwell. . . . For surely, O LORD, you bless the righteous; you surround them with your favor as with a shield.

PSALM 5:4,12

I have a great respect for those who serve in the military. Perhaps it goes back to my high school days when the boys in our class were called to active duty to fight a war in Korea. I went on to college but dropped out one summer to do my patriotic duty by working in Washington, D.C., for the Navy. There I got a closer perspective on the horror of war.

I have listened to uncles and cousins and brothers relate their personal war stories. One barely survived the Bataan Death March, where some 67,000 Allied prisoners died.[1] These stories and others have placed a soft spot in my heart for all those who serve.

In recent years, as I've spoken on military bases both in this country and overseas, I've developed an even deeper appreciation for those who serve as sentinels for our freedom.

I vividly remember one first of May when I found myself in Japan on a U.S. base gathered around 50 American flags that snapped in the high wind. The occasion was the National Day of Prayer for America.

I was a visitor, just one in the crowd composed of members of a military band, choirs, school children and servicemen with their families who met to pray for our nation. As we sang "God bless America, land that I love . . . ," a knot formed in my throat in gratitude to God for my homeland and for the men and women stationed here.

As I approached the platform to give the history of the National Day of Prayer, I felt privileged to participate in this service. This base, I was told, had been used by Japanese pilots in World War II to train kamikaze pilots who would commit suicide to extinguish the enemy. Now we stood on what was no longer enemy territory, praying for our own nation. And I'm sure some were praying silently for our host nation, too.

GOOD NIGHT, LORD

Today, Lord, when I sat next to a serviceman, I told him how much I appreciated his sacrifice for our country and that I pray for our military men and women. He looked at me in disbelief. No one had ever told him they pray for military personnel. Then he asked me not to stop praying. Lord, I am so indebted to those who are dedicated to defending our country. Bless and protect them; watch over their families and draw them all closer, still closer to You. In Jesus' name I pray. Amen.

Note
1. *Webster's New World Encyclopedia* (New York: Prentice Hall, 1993), p. 110.

Spiritual Weapons of Authority

Put on God's whole armor . . . that you may be able successfully to stand up against [all] the strategies and the deceits of the devil.

EPHESIANS 6:11, AMP

When I'm in the prayer gap for someone, I see myself standing between God and that person, pleading on his or her behalf; at the same time I am standing between Satan and that person, battling on his or her behalf.

Jesus taught His followers a model for prayer that includes: "And lead us not into temptation, but deliver us from the evil one" (Matt. 6:13). In His great priestly prayer for His followers, Jesus asked the Father to "protect them from the evil one" (John 17:15).

Paul later wrote to Christians, exhorting them to stand firm against the schemes of the devil because "our struggle is not against flesh and blood, but against the rulers, against the authorities, against the powers of this dark world and against the spiritual forces of evil in the heavenly realms" (Eph. 6:12).

The sacrificial death, burial and resurrection of Jesus is the basis of our victory over Satan. After His resurrection, Christ delegated to us His authority over the devil and his evil cohorts. Yet we must be motivated to use His power if we want to see results.

Consider what Jesus taught His followers: "I will give you the keys of the kingdom of heaven; whatever you bind on earth will be bound in heaven, and whatever you loose on earth will be loosed in heaven" (Matt. 16:19).

He also says, "No one can enter a strong man's house and plunder his goods, unless he first binds the strong man. And then he will plunder his house" (Mark 3:27, NKJV).

To bind evil spirits means to restrain them by addressing them directly and forbidding them to continue their destructive activity. Through the power of the Holy Spirit, our words can help loose someone from the enemy's bondage. In prayer we ask the Holy Spirit to minister to his or her need. Our prayer is directed to God, our warfare at the enemy.[1]

Remember when Jesus was tempted by the devil during His wilderness experience? He spoke directly to the enemy and said, "Begone, Satan! For it is written . . . ," and He quoted the Word of God (see Matt. 4:10). Quoting the Word of God is a great way for *us* to attack the enemy, too.

God will give us weapons of warfare to fight our particular battles if we are familiar with the Bible and if we are alert when He instructs us.

GOOD NIGHT, LORD

Lord, teach me how to be attentive to Your voice so that when I need spiritual weapons and strategy I will be properly equipped. I don't want to ever move in presumption but rather to totally rely on the leading of the Holy Spirit and the Word of God!

Note
1. From *How to Pray for Your Family and Friends,* © 1990 by Quin Sherrer and Ruthanne Garlock. Published by Servant Publications, Ann Arbor, Michigan, p. 131. Used with permission.

Safeguard Your Home

The graven images of their gods you are to burn with fire. . . . And you shall not bring an abomination into your house, and like it come under the ban; you shall utterly detest it and you shall utterly abhor it, for it is something banned.

DEUTERONOMY 7:25,26, NASB

I was visiting a friend's home when she had a dream in the night that her son was hiding pornography in the house. She believed her dream was a warning from God.

The next morning, while I prayed beside her, she took a flashlight and searched until she found his stack of magazines. Then she destroyed them. Because he was still living under her roof, she believed she had the authority and responsibility before God to cleanse her house of evil.

All of us can safeguard our homes by taking some important steps, depending on where we are in our Christian walk.

First, we can *commit our homes to the Lord* by anointing the doors and doorposts with oil as an outward symbol that we are dedicating our home to God and petitioning Him for the safety of those who dwell there.

Second, *we can pray over our family members at night,* asking God for their health and safety, even if we do it after they are asleep.

Third, *we can remove from our homes and destroy* any pornographic, New Age or occult toys, games, music, videos, disks, books, posters and any artifacts associated with false religions, cults or occult practices—any of Satan's counterfeit guises or anything that gives glory to violence.

Fourth, *we can ask the Holy Spirit to reveal any specific spirits to be cast out* (see Mark 9:25). Address any and all spirits associated with any objectionable things that once were in the house. Command them to depart in the name and authority of Jesus

Christ, and remind them they have no right to remain.

The Bible gives a brief account of the Early Church in Ephesus, showing what happened when Paul addressed issues of occult practices:

> Many also of those who had believed kept coming, confessing and disclosing their practices. And many of those who practiced magic brought their books together and began burning them in the sight of all; and they counted up the price of them and found it fifty thousand pieces of silver (Acts 19:18,19, *NASB*).

Women who are married to unbelievers are not necessarily free to destroy things that belong to their husbands or in-laws, though they know the items are an abomination to the Lord. But they can, in the name of Jesus Christ, bind the spirits associated with those objects, in the name and power of Jesus Christ, and remind them that they have no right to remain.

When it comes to our children, we can keep them from listening to rock music or watching occult shows on TV. They are under our authority until the legal age of adulthood and subject to us while they live in our homes. We must take this seriously if we want our homes cleansed.[1]

GOOD NIGHT, LORD

Lord, continue to show me if there are things I need to rid my home of so that it will be a cleansed vessel to bring You glory. Amen.

Note
1. From *A Woman's Guide to Breaking Bondages*, © 1994 by Quin Sherrer and Ruthanne Garlock. Published by Servant Publications, Ann Arbor, Michigan, p. 172. Used with permission.

Prayers for Our Children

Be joyful always; pray continually; give thanks in all circumstances,
for this is God's will for you in Christ Jesus.

1 THESSALONIANS 5:16-18

Beyond dedicating our children to the Lord, forgiving them and loving them unconditionally, we can pray for them to have godly goals.

It's never too early to begin doing this! It's good to plant "waiting prayers"—praying for your children's future while they are still young. Naturally, we have to wait for answers to some of these prayers.

A wise gardener plants his seeds and then has the good sense not to dig them up every few days to see if a crop is on the way. Likewise, we must be patient as God brings the answers to our waiting prayers in His own good time.

Of course, we also pray for the various phases of our children's lives.

One effective way to pray is to personalize verses of Scripture, such as replacing the pronouns with the names of the children for whom you are interceding. For example, Psalm 23:3 could be personalized in this way: "Thank You, Lord, that You guide my son, Keith, in paths of righteousness for Your name's sake."

Another way to personalize Scripture is to speak it aloud about your child. "My child, (insert name), will be found to have a keen mind and knowledge and understanding and ability to solve difficult problems. He/she does have wisdom and insight and breadth of understanding as measureless as the sand on the seashore" (see Dan. 2:14, 5:12; 1 Kings 4:29).

Here are further Scripture suggestions you might want to consider:

1. Pray that Jesus Christ be formed in your children (see Gal. 4:19).
2. Pray that your children—the seed of the righteous—will be delivered from the evil one (see Prov. 11:21 *KJV*; Matt. 6:13).
3. Pray that your children will be taught by the Lord and that their peace will be great (see Isa. 54:13)
4. Pray that they will learn to discern good from evil and have a good conscience toward God (see Heb. 5:14; 1 Peter 3:21).
5. Pray that God's laws will be in their minds and on their hearts (see Heb. 8:10).
6. Pray that they will choose companions who are wise— not fools, nor sexually immoral, nor drunkards, nor idolaters, nor slanderers, nor swindlers (see Prov. 13:20; 1 Cor. 5:11).
7. Pray that they will remain sexually pure and keep themselves only for their spouses, asking God for His grace to keep such a commitment (see Eph. 5:3,31-33).
8. Pray that they will honor their parents (see Eph. 6:1-3).[1]

Let's consider how you might pray for a child who is being adversely influenced by peers. God may lead you to pray as David did when he believed his son Absalom was hearing the wrong advice. He asked the Lord to "turn [the] counsel into foolishness" (2 Sam. 15:31).

The Lord may lead you to pray that your child be "delivered from wicked and evil men" and that God would "strengthen and protect [him/her] from the evil one" (2 Thess. 3:2,3).

God may want you to bless the person your child is listening to, even when your natural inclination is to ask God to remove that harmful influence from your child's life. You can pray that God will accomplish His plan and purpose in that person, bringing the right people into his or her life at the right time (see Eph. 1:11; Matt. 9:38). God broke Job's captivity when he prayed for his friends (see Job 42:10), and they weren't exactly the kind of friends most of us would want.

God may give you many other Scriptures to pray for your children. Here are some you might want to read aloud for encouragement when your children are not as spiritually fit as they could be:

> Do not be afraid, for I am with you; I will bring your children from the east and gather you from the west. I will say to the north, "Give them up!" and to the south, "Do not hold them back." Bring my sons from afar and my daughters from the ends of the earth—everyone who is called by my name, whom I created for my glory, whom I formed and made (Isa. 43:5-7).

> This is what the LORD says: "Restrain your voice from weeping and your eyes from tears, for your work will be rewarded," declares the LORD. "They will return from the land of the enemy. So there is hope for your future," declares the LORD. "Your children will return to their own land" (Jer. 31:16,17).

GOOD NIGHT, LORD

Tonight, heavenly Father, I'm grateful for the many ways You have allowed us to be encouraged by Scriptures in the Bible so that we can make many of them our prayers for our children. Tonight I can think of no better way to bring my children to You than to pray the powerful prayer Jesus taught His disciples.

"Our Father who are in heaven, hallowed be thy name, your kingdom come, your will be done on earth as it is in heaven. Give us today our daily bread. Forgive us our debts, as we also have forgiven our debtors. And lead us not into temptation, but deliver us from the evil one" (Matt. 6:9-13). *Amen.*

Note
1. Quin Sherrer and Ruthanne Garlock, *How to Pray for Your Children* (Ventura, Calif.: Regal Books, 1998), pp. 33, 34.

Me, a Coward?

O LORD my God, I called to you for help and you healed me.

PSALM 30:2

I think I became a coward when I became a parent. The first time I had to surrender my baby—only eight months old—into the hands of a surgeon, I almost panicked.

As a mother of three, I often had reason for my heart to quiver, my brow to sweat and my eyes to get teary.

The first broken tooth, the first suture just above the eye, the first X-rays of a skull, a broken arm from a backyard football game, a hospital stay for the son dehydrated from working too long in the Florida sun. Or the ambulance ride and emergency-room treatment when his car was hit by a careless driver.

Somewhere in between the dangerously high fevers and flu, eye surgery, getting broken bones set and more, I came to dread trips to the hospital.

But how I loved those doctors and nurses when they said, "All's well." How fervently I thanked God!

Now we've just experienced the agony of watching our two-year-old granddaughter Victoria Jewett suffer with pneumonia in both lungs for five long days in the hospital, piped oxygen assisting her breathing. My husband lost a brother at her age from the same malady, so I'm particularly grateful for modern medicines, treatments and all her medical caregivers. I'm also thankful for the many prayer warriors who joined us in 'round-the-clock prayer for her life.

Her four-year-old brother, who stayed with me, stopped his play several times a day to pray for his Sissy. When she was finally able to breathe without the oxygen tubes and allowed to come

home, he jumped up and down, saying, "It's a miracle, a miracle!"
I was inclined to agree. God and the doctors had done a fine job.

GOOD NIGHT, LORD

Lord, I acknowledge You as the Great Physician. Without Your divine guidance and Your healing touch, no doctor could do a medical miracle. Tonight I want to thank You for those who labor in the fields of medicine and science to help stamp out disease and develop new techniques for treating infections. Keep them from weariness and help them stay keen and alert. Show me ways to express my appreciation to them. I so deeply respect doctors, nurses and medical technicians who work with compassion, using their skills to help our bodies mend. Amen.

Something to Cherish

Dear friends, do not be surprised at the painful trial you are suffering, as though something strange were happening to you. But rejoice that you participate in the sufferings of Christ, so that you may be overjoyed when his glory is revealed.

1 PETER 4:12-13

I had been Mom's caregiver for more than a year. Now she was losing her battle with cancer. We'd read every Scripture we could find on healing, health and heaven. We suspected she was about to enter into her eternal reward in heaven, with the Savior she loved so much.

Though Mom hadn't spoken in days, I continued to speak to her as though she understood. The visiting nurse had said she was in a semi-comatose state. Early on the morning of my birthday, I spoke to her as usual. "Mom, I love you. I'm going to say the Lord's Prayer again this morning. You just agree with me." I prayed aloud and then repeated Psalm 23 as I always did this time of the morning. I cranked the rented hospital bed higher to reposition her.

"I'll be right back," I reassured her. Then I turned on a cassette tape recording of her favorite choruses and hymns and slipped out of the room to get a cup of coffee. I hummed along with the music.

Just as I reached the kitchen I heard her yell something. "Why, she hasn't said a thing in days," I told my sister Ann, who was visiting to help me with Mom. We both ran back to Mom's room. The melody on her tape player was the chorus whose first line is "Open my eyes, Lord, I want to see Jesus."

We watched as through clenched teeth she gave a weak shout, "Hallelujah! Hallelujah! Hallelujah!" That was all. A faint smile played across her face. Still she showed no recognition of us. Had she seen a glimpse of heaven? Then I remembered what the social services nurse had told me a few weeks earlier: "You'll be glad you took her home from the hospital and not to a nursing home. I'm sure she will say or do something so special, you'll always cherish the moment."

A few days later, just after Easter, Mom died in her own bedroom. Ann and I were there. I could only rejoice. The victory was won. A saint had entered heaven.

When I told several close friends when my mother had died, I learned that some had at that very moment heard God's gentle voice ask them to pray for her—escorting her in prayer into the heavenlies.

Two prayer warriors, Fran and Effie, from Mom's prayer group in Destin, Florida, gathered in a home to pray specifically for her as she was breathing her last. Carol stopped her housework and went to walk on the beach beside the wave-tossed surf to intercede for her. Laura, 450 miles away in Melbourne, Florida, put down the manuscript she was writing and walked out onto her screen porch to pray for her. Aunt Betty in California—clear across the States— picked up her Bible and said a special prayer for her.

All this went on at the moment Mom was entering heaven. How comforting to me to learn that God had spoken to each of these women in His quiet way and asked them to stop and pray for her.[1]

At her funeral, the congregation in her little Episcopal church sang the words, "Christ the Lord is risen today, hallelujah!"

I hope that when my toughest time on earth comes, I can say with Mom, "Lord, give me grace to endure. I want this to be an opportunity, not an ordeal."

The Bible says there is a time to die. Each of us will face death someday. Can we, will we, be ready to meet our Lord with no regrets?

GOOD NIGHT, LORD

Thank You, Lord, that You gave me some precious moments to cherish as I cared for Mom in her home during her last days of suffering. Especially do I cherish her shouting "Hallelujah" on my birthday—her final words spoken this side of heaven. Such an assurance of her love for You and of her final destination. Thank You for the dear friends who stood in the prayer gap as she was ready to enter Your gates with thanksgiving. Help me to be as brave a soldier as she when my time comes to depart this earth. Amen.

Note

1. From *Listen, God Is Speaking to You,* © 1999 by Quin Sherrer. Published by Servant Publications, Ann Arbor, Michigan, pp. 121, 122. Used with permission.

Stretcher Bearer for God

Do not forsake your friend and the friend of your father.

PROVERBS 27:10

At any moment in life, any one of us can suddenly need a stretcher bearer. When we find ourselves emotionally drained, spiritually dry or physically ill, how we need someone to encourage and support us!

Like the paralytic's caring friends, who loved enough to take him to Jesus to receive wholeness, there will be times when we too may need such friends. Or when we need to be that carrier for others.

Yes, we can go to Him alone. But God's Word also admonishes us to love, to encourage, to pray for and to bear one another's burdens. In fact, there are more than 50 "one another," or reciprocal, commands in the Bible.

Sometimes you may feel like you're the only one in the pressure cooker. The only one hurting. The only one with children under fire. The only one with a husband without work. The only one needing help!

A pastor once rescued a teenager who was drowning off the coast of California. When he asked the teen why he didn't cry out for help, the young man replied, "What would my friends think?" Pride, stubbornness, fear of peer pressure—these almost cost him his life. But God had stationed a pastor and his family on the beach to be a rescuer, a stretcher bearer.

You and I can make a difference in this world—not because of what we do for the Lord, but because of what He will do through us when we yield to Him.

GOOD NIGHT, LORD

Lord, help me to be more sensitive to encourage and build up a friend—especially one going through a tough time. I want to make a difference in the lives of those You put in my path. Teach me how to be so tuned to their troubles that I can be a stretcher bearer for You. Help me to recognize when Your assignment is for me to pray for them. Or take them a pot of soup. Or baby-sit. Or just send a card of encouragement. Thank You for those people You have sent to help me when I was the one in need. Lord, I am willing for You to wake me in the night to intercede for someone going through a trial—just place that person on my heart. Amen.

Releasing a Friend on Earth

Jesus said . . . , "I am the resurrection and the life. He who believes in me will live, even though he dies; and whoever lives and believes in me will never die."

JOHN 11:25,26

One of the brain tumors is inoperable—as are other tumors in his body. This long-time friend of ours lies in a hospital bed at home. He's been through surgery, chemotherapy and dozens of trips back and forth to the hospital.

His wife wrote: "God is so good. Without the church support and prayers of friends, I don't think I could get through all of this. We don't have a lot of hope his body will survive. However, his soul is right with God and he loves the Lord Jesus Christ with his whole heart."

We've come a long distance to see him. He recognizes us but cannot speak. We kneel beside his bed to pray—his wife, my husband and I. We commit him into God's care.

There is a time to be born and a time to die. How hard it is to release a friend we love so much. But what gladness to know he has an eternal home waiting because he has a personal relationship with Jesus.

GOOD NIGHT, LORD

Lord, I sit with my friend as we watch life slowly ebb from her husband. The brain tumors are winning out. But how he loves You! How he loves his wife, his "sweetie." He knows when we're praying, and though he cannot speak, he prays along with us, squeezing our hands, blinking his eyes, even crying. We trust You to know the exact time for his homegoing—for his safekeeping in heaven. Father, into Your hands we commit his spirit. Prepare and comfort his family. Give them strength and wisdom for what lies ahead. His wife has been under such an umbrella of Your peace and grace. Keep her there even after her loss. I thank You for touching the whole family with Your love. In Jesus' name. Amen.

Prayerwalking

[Jesus speaking:] " *'Love the Lord your God with all your heart and with all your soul and with all your mind and with all your strength.' The second is this: 'Love your neighbor as yourself.' There is no commandment greater than these."*

MARK 12:30,31

One way we Christian women can help fulfill the Great Commission is by praying through our neighborhoods on a regular basis.

To the ordinary observer I am pulling my grandchildren in a little red wagon through a three-block area in our neighborhood. But in reality we are on a "prayerwalk."

As we go down the sidewalk, we'll sing, sometimes making up verses to go with popular tunes they already know. Often all we do is sing "Hallelujah" in front of each home. I may offer a short prayer and they add their "Amen." They are learning that prayer can take place outside our home or church and that we really care for neighbors.

What is prayerwalking? In their book *Prayerwalking,* Steve Hawthorne and Graham Kendrick explain:

> Prayerwalking is on-site prayer—simply praying in the very places where you expect your prayers to be answered.
>
> Walking helps sensitize you to the realities of your community. Sounds, sights and smells, far from distracting your prayer, engage both body and mind in the art of praying. Better perception means boosted intercession.
>
> Walking also connects Christians with their own neighborhoods. By regularly passing through the streets

to their cities, walkers can present an easygoing accessibility to neighbors. Walking seems to create opportunities to help or to pray for new friends on the spot, right at the times of great need. Some streets present risks, but vulnerability yields valuable contact with those who have yet to follow Christ.[1]

In light of recent street violence in some of our cities, we must keep alert, asking God where and when we are to prayerwalk and with whom. Sometimes neighborhood women ban together for this activity.

My friend Mary takes literally Jesus' command to "love your neighbor as yourself." As she walks on her street, she makes it a habit to proclaim: "Lord, we invite the King of Glory to come in. Come forth and bring Your glory into this neighborhood. Release Your blessings to the families here."

One of her neighborhood's most successful events is called "Meet You at the Corner." The neighbors gather on a Saturday morning before Easter for a short service, declaring "He is alive!" They share refreshments and fellowship. Even the children come along with their parents.

Experienced intercessors suggest these preliminary steps before you begin prayerwalking in your neighborhood or city:

- Prepare your heart with the Lord. Is it free of judgments, hatred, envy?
- Evaluate your neighborhood (or city) by knowing history or the layout. Don't take on too much territory all at once. Mary suggests walking several streets but picking only one to five families to pray for on a regular basis during your devotional time at home.
- Ask God for His purpose and vision for your prayerwalk.

- Seek God for guidance on what Scriptures you are to proclaim as you walk. Memorize Scriptures that you can say aloud, declaring God's love for your neighbors and city.[2]

We need to give God thanks for our city and neighbors, standing with them in repentance, crying out for mercy and extending God's blessing on them.

GOOD NIGHT, LORD

Lord, help me reach out to my neighbors. I want to know how to pray more effectively. I want to be a good Samaritan in bringing them to You. Whether they are next door, at the grocery store, at my workplace or wherever our paths cross, help me to be Your hands extended. Bless my neighbors today, I ask in Jesus' name. Amen.

Notes
1. Steve Hawthorne and Graham Kenrick, *Prayerwalking* (Orlando, Fla.: Creation House, 1993), pp. 15-17.
2. From *A Woman's Guide to Spirit-Filled Living*, © 1996 by Quin Sherrer and Ruthanne Garlock. Published by Servant Publications, Ann Arbor, Michigan, pp. 228, 229. Used with permission.

Praying for Unsaved Friends

It is true that I am an ordinary, weak human being, but I don't use human plans
and methods to win my battles. I use God's mighty weapons, not those made by
men, to knock down the devil's strongholds. These weapons can break down
every proud argument against God and every wall that can be built to keep men
from finding him. With these weapons I can capture rebels and bring them back
to God, and change them into men whose hearts' desire is obedience to Christ.

2 CORINTHIANS 10:3-5, TLB

"Without God, we cannot. Without us, God will not." St. Augustine's succinct statement sums up the twofold nature of intercession.

God empowers us by the Holy Spirit to intercede for others' needs. Without that empowerment our prayers would be empty words.

God also invests us with Christ's authority to restrain satanic forces that are blinding and hindering the person for whom we are praying. God could restrain those forces without our participation if He chose to. But He has equipped us and commissioned us to intercede by pushing back the enemy, thus allowing the Holy Spirit to bring conviction that leads to repentance.[1]

While we don't have authority over a person's will, we recognize that God has given His believers authority in the spirit realm to pray and help rescue those caught in the enemy's grip.

My friend has plunged into a very dangerous lifestyle. Some of her strongholds are mind-sets or conclusions contrary to Scripture—often they are lies the devil has whispered to her. My role is to continually pray that the walls that keep her from finding Jesus will come down in His mighty name.

Today as I read a paraphrase of what Paul said to the Christians in Corinth, I felt a new anointing to pray more specifically and with more authority.

Here are some specific Scriptures you might pray for unsaved friends and loved ones: Matthew 18:12-14; Acts 26:18; 2 Corinthians 4:3-6; 10:4,5; 2 Timothy 2:25,26; 2 Peter 3:8,9.

GOOD NIGHT, LORD

Heavenly Father, I come to You tonight, standing in the prayer gap on behalf of my friend_____(name). May she be delivered from spiritual blindness and from every scheme and snare the devil has used to hold her captive. Let every stronghold of unbelief and vain imagination in her life be pulled down and brought into captivity to the obedience of Christ. Speak to her by the Holy Spirit, revealing to her that she must call upon You to be saved, and give her a desire to do it. I pray for people to come across her path who will share the gospel with her. May her heart be softened to respond to Your love. I pray this in the name of Your Son, Jesus! Amen.

Note
1. From *The Spiritual Warrior's Prayer Guide*, © 1992 by Quin Sherrer and Ruthanne Garlock. Published by Servant Publications, Ann Arbor, Michigan, pp. 223. Used with permission.

Broken Marriage

But if the unbeliever leaves, let him do so. A believing man or woman is not bound in such circumstances; God has called us to live in peace.

1 CORINTHIANS 7:15

Too many marriages are coming apart. The statistics are alarming. So many hearts are breaking. Tonight I bring to God my concern for a special friend—a coworker who has blessed my life.

GOOD NIGHT, LORD

Dear Lord, help my friend Lynn adjust to separation. It's hard to give up a man who has been a part of your life for 15 years or even for five.

She tries to forget the quarrels, fights, butting together of personalities. Their love has withered. The relationship has hit a deadlock. It seems unlikely that it can be salvaged. He has another love in his life.

He refuses to see a counselor. He has never gone to church with her. He controls her with an upper hand—even confiscating her own paycheck from work. Manipulation. Emotional abuse. Oh, God, how I ache for her.

Keep her from plunging off that jagged mountain ledge into further despair, heartbreak and aloneness. Lord, help her to overcome this depression.

My friend is hurting so much tonight. Please give her Your wisdom concerning what steps to take next. She needs You so much. As she cries herself to sleep, comfort and love on her, my Savior. She knows You and she's asked me to pray. In Jesus name, I ask this. Amen.

Dying Without the Savior

For God so loved the world that he gave his one and only Son, that whoever believes in him shall not perish but have eternal life.

JOHN 3:16

She has no living children. Married more than 50 years. Now she's lying in a coma in a hospital and could die at any moment.

I've been crying out to God to speak to her—even in her coma. For a vision. Or angels. Or even the Lord Himself to come remind her of the commitment she made as a child when she acknowledged Jesus as her Savior.

I've stood over her bed with other relatives as we've read aloud from the Bible and the *Book of Common Prayer.* We've committed her spirit to the Lord. We've asked Him to forgive her sins. We've begged that in some way He will touch her spirit. Now that she can't communicate with us, we won't know if or how He did it. But we know He can.

Years ago, for some reason unknown to us, she turned her back on Him. She'd usually laugh when I tried to speak of God's love for her. Was it a mocking laugh or just a cover-up for the fact that she couldn't believe He could love her personally? I've pondered these questions often.

How sad to deliberately refuse His offer of life forever with Him—to die without the Savior. My heart is broken.

A lot of Christians have family members who have turned their backs on Christ. We need to remember that God gave man free will, the option to say yes or no to His great gift.

For 20 years my friend Cynthia prayed for her mom to become a Christian. Then, during the last weeks of her mother's illness, Cynthia stood over her bed, begging her to accept the Lord. But there was no answer.

Three days before her death, Cynthia's mom told her, "He came to me. He said it was a gift."

"He is the gift, Mom. You don't have to work to earn a place in heaven. If you would only ask Jesus into your heart, you would experience His comfort. He's here to help you."

Cynthia's mom wouldn't answer. Her silence was deafening. But soon afterwards, during one episode of intense pain, she gasped, "Jesus, come into my heart. Forgive me for my sins. Lord, I take the gift. I take the gift from You. Thank You." She died as she was holding her daughter's hand.

Cynthia says, "I told her if she would look into His eyes she would see His kindness, His gentleness. She would be with Him, no longer suffering in this world."

What a comfort to know her mom is safe in His care!

GOOD NIGHT, LORD

Dear Lord, I cry out for Your mercy for my relative. Somehow, even while she's in a coma, will You come to her and draw her to Yourself? Remind her of her one-time walk with You. Forgive her for the bitterness and hate she let enter her thought life. Forgive her for all the regrets and disappointments in life she constantly talked about. Lord, while I am sad that she's about to depart this life, I'm even sadder that the last time I talked to her she was separated from You. Come, Lord Jesus, and woo this wounded lamb back to Yourself. I know nothing is impossible with You. Amen.

Call for Help

Call to me and I will answer you and tell you great and
unsearchable things you do not know.

JEREMIAH 33:3

I watched her in the Atlanta airport—the woman with the tiny package covered with a white cloth. She'd taken the cover off for a moment and I saw the bird.

The woman was one of the first to board the plane. I couldn't help but notice that she pushed the little box under her seat and took out a magazine to read. Before long I heard a creepy little voice say, "Help me! Help me! Help me!"

To the airline attendant it sounded like an elderly passenger in need of help. She roamed up and down the aisle looking for the voice. The lady with the box hidden in front of her seat never let on it was her talking bird crying out.

I listened to that silly cry so long that when we landed, I greeted my husband with a squawky, "Help me. Help me. Help me." I giggled as he looked at me strangely and grabbed my luggage.

How many times have I come to God like that? "Help me. Help me," I cry. But I fail to acknowledge that He is more than willing to help me if I'd only let Him. He knows where I am and how I need Him. He's always there. But He wants a two-way conversation with me, not just my cries for help.

GOOD NIGHT, LORD

Lord, forgive me for not giving You time to speak to me. Forgive me for being so busy that all I want to do is call out "Help!" Thank You that You are a forever God, always near, always listening, always wanting to talk to me, too. I do cherish our talk-times! But Lord, at times today I got distracted with all the other voices, sounds and sights around me. I'm sorry for not tuning in to You more devotedly. In Jesus' name, I pray. Amen.

God Longs to Speak to Us

Therefore consider carefully how you listen.

LUKE 8:18

Most of us, if we're honest, have a longing to hear God speak to us directly and personally. We want our prayers answered and our lives touched by His hand. We desire His guidance and protection. We want Him to reveal the meaning behind the mysteries of our lives and to use us to touch others' lives.

Maybe we think He won't speak to little people like us. Or perhaps we have too narrow a view of how He speaks today. We tend to box Him in with our limited expectations. When the signs we hope for don't come, we think that He's not listening or that He doesn't care.

The truth is, God is always trying to speak to us. When we let go of our preconceived notions of *how* He speaks, *when* He speaks and *to whom* He speaks and simply listen with childlike faith, we will be surprised at how readily we can hear His voice. He is with us at every turn. He uses everything and anything to call us to Himself.

Instead of a direct, audible voice thundering from heaven, God's Holy Spirit often speaks into our hearts. The Holy Spirit not only speaks, He guides us, reveals the things of God, strengthens and encourages us, convicts us of sin and loves through us.[1]

Sometimes God speaks through ordinary events. When we ask Him to guide our steps and guard our thoughts, we can count on Him to give us answers to decisions in the routine things of life. He may send us a vision, a dream, a circumstance or even a person to speak into a situation in our life.

Sometimes our Creator uses nature to communicate with us—when we take a walk through the woods, a stroll on the beach or a boat ride on a lake or when we watch a thousand snowflakes fall outside our window. He speaks to others in solitude, during complete silence. Still others set aside times to fast in order to hear Him more clearly. Some of us, myself included, like to hear Him while soaking in the tub or enjoying an invigorating shower.

Those who relate well to music may hear God's voice as a message through a song that plays over and over in their thoughts. Some hear Him as they listen to worship music, the words of a song penetrating deep within their spirit with a special directive from God.[2]

When we really want to know someone well, don't we spend time with him or her? We listen, ask for an opinion, observe reactions. In the same way, we get to know God better by spending time with Him. Reading and studying the Bible are critical, since these are the primary means He uses to speak to us about who He is and how He want us to live.

God speaks in these and many other ways. If we are open to hearing His voice at every turn, we will begin to recognize it with much greater frequency.[3]

GOOD NIGHT, LORD

Lord, thank You that You still yearn to speak to us today. You can do it through a still, small voice, through a Bible passage, through a friend or through a thought You drop into my mind. Lord, give me discernment to know which is Your voice, which is my own and which is the voice of the enemy. I invite the Holy Spirit to teach me. I ask this in Jesus' name. Amen.

Notes

1. From *Listen, God Is Speaking to You,* © 1999 by Quin Sherrer. Published by Servant Publications, Ann Arbor, Michigan, p. 22. Used with permission.
2. Ibid., p. 186.
3. Ibid., pp. 25, 26.

Neighborhood, City and Nation

The LORD said, "If I find fifty righteous people in the city of Sodom, I will spare the whole place for their sake." Then Abraham spoke up. . . . "What if only ten can be found there?" He answered, "For the sake of ten, I will not destroy it."

GENESIS 18:26,27,32

Have you ever felt as if you were living in exile? A place where you just didn't like or identify with the community or neighborhood? Where you were only existing—enduring—but not calling it home?

I've been there, too. But one day when I was having a pity party because my husband had moved us so far away from family and friends—where the norm was dust storms in spring and blizzards in winter—I found a Scripture to help me: "Seek the peace and prosperity of the city to which I have carried you into exile. Pray to the LORD for it, because if it prospers, you too will prosper" (Jer. 29:7).

So I had a new assignment—to pray for the peace and prosperity of the city where we were now living. I asked God to give me a better appreciation for this place and, if He would, even a love for it. And I prayed for it.

Just as I was settling down and believing I could live there indefinitely, a job opportunity opened up back in Florida where we'd once lived. So we happily packed up and moved back "home," this time bringing a newborn Texan with us.

In the years that have passed, I've learned that prayer can be a proclamation to our neighborhoods and cities, releasing God's word of redemption throughout the nation. God exhorts us to pray for the peace and prosperity of the city and region where we live. He also directs some individual intercessors to pray for cities and nations where their feet may never walk. In prayer we can "possess the land," so to speak, calling for God's purposes to be fulfilled and the gospel proclaimed in those areas.

When we recognize that the enemy blinds people to the truth of the gospel, we pray in an attempt to tear down strongholds of deception and unbelief, enabling them to hear and believe the Word of God. The apostle Paul wrote: "And even if our gospel is veiled, it is veiled to those who are perishing. The god of this age has blinded the minds of unbelievers, so that they cannot see the light of the gospel of the glory of Christ" (2 Cor. 4:3,4).

Once we understand how evil forces are hindering God's work, believers have the authority to break the control of those spirits through prayer and fasting. First, we declare we have the blood of Jesus over us before we engage in spiritual battle. After getting God's strategy through prayer, we may then need to pull down strongholds that keep people in bondage. Perhaps we'll begin to recognize some of these, such as greed, independence, poverty and steeped tradition that keep people blinded.[1]

We are also admonished to pray for all those in authority so that "we may lead a quiet and peaceable life in all godliness and reverence" (1 Tim. 2:2, NKJV). One commentator wrote, "We must pray for those who are in authority over us if we wish to reap the benefits of good government, which is a prized gift from God for the church's welfare and advancement of the gospel."[2] That tells me I should spend some time praying for leaders at various governmental levels—that they would have wisdom beyond their experience to lead and govern us in righteousness.

I'm still learning how important it is for each of us to stand in the prayer gap for the territory God lays on our hearts. We may feel called to pray for our city, our neighborhood, our nation or even another country.

GOOD NIGHT, LORD

Lord, I am so selfish sometimes, praying only for me, mine and ours. Keep me sensitive to travail in prayer until spiritual revival comes to my neighborhood and any other territory You lay on my heart. Lord, I pray for peace in our neighborhood. I ask for Your intervention. I pray that those who don't know You will come to a knowledge of Jesus Christ. In His name I pull down idolatry, pride, greed, deception, immorality, hatred, division, humanism and false religions from our neighborhood. I call forth that which is Your nature, Father, which is to do justice, love mercy and walk in humility. I cry out for Your Spirit to be manifested among us. I ask all this in the name of the Son of God, Jesus Christ. Amen.

Notes

1. From *The Spiritual Warrior's Prayer Guide*, © 1992 by Quin Sherrer and Ruthanne Garlock. Published by Servant Publications, Ann Arbor, Michigan, pp. 273-276. Used with permission.
2. *The Spirit-Filled Life Bible, NKJV* (Nashville, Tenn.: Thomas Nelson Publishers, 1991), p. 1842.

A Significant Time

There is a time for everything,

and a season for every activity under heaven:

a time to be born and a time to die,

a time to plant and a time to uproot,

a time to kill and a time to heal,

a time to tear down and a time to build,

a time to weep and a time to laugh.

ECCLESIASTES 3:1-4

Most of us have read this passage in Ecclesiastes and quote it, saying, "There is a time for everything." The word "time" has two Greek meanings in the New Testament. *Kairos* is a succession of moments. The other word for time is *chronos*—the passage of time with no special significance.[1]

Kairos time could be, for example, a special meeting with someone that God arranged for us, maybe to change a direction in our life or as a confirmation through that person that we are already taking the right course. It could be what some people call a "divine appointment."

Sometimes we miss His timing. Maybe we didn't accept a certain invitation because we were just too tired. Yet God had a special event waiting for us. We didn't inquire of Him first whether we should go. We didn't ask and we didn't listen.

Kairos time is better understood as an opportune time—to be where God wants us to be at a precise time or talking to certain people at a specific locality. Have you ever had what you thought was a chance meeting with a stranger or acquaintance? Later you thought, *Wow, that was God-arranged. I needed that.* Or maybe you took some action that turned out for your good to such an extent that you just knew you had been in

God's perfect will and timing. That's kairos!

A friend of mine tried for years to share the gospel with her elderly aunt who always got mad when anyone talked about God. She didn't need salvation, she'd tell them. She had lived a moral life. She was a good person.

One day my friend left a book of prayers with her, fully expecting another tongue-lashing. She knew the book contained a prayer of repentance from sins and words to use to accept Jesus as Lord.

The next day when she dropped by to visit, her aunt told her, "I read the book you left me. I want you to know I now have my reservation in the Upper Room." Kairos timing! The niece had never heard anyone call heaven the "upper room," but she knew her aunt had an experience with the Lord when she asked for more Christian books.

How God wants us to be alert to the golden opportunities He gives us—as individuals, as a nation, as a generation! In the Bible we read about a beautiful Jewish woman named Esther who became queen of Persia "for such a time as this" and whose actions of intervention helped save her people (see the book of Esther).

When Abraham and Sarah had waited many years for a child, God's promise was: "At the appointed [kairos] time . . . Sarah will have a son" (Rom. 9:9). And she did.

Old Simeon waited years for his kairos time, for God promised he would not die until he had seen the Messiah. When he saw the Christ child, he told God he was now ready to die. Anna, the prophetess, who waited with fasting and prayers for her kairos time in the Temple, saw the baby Jesus, too. Afterwards she spoke to all who were looking forward to the redemption of Jerusalem, which makes me think she left the Temple to proclaim that the Messiah had come! (See Luke 2:22-38.)

God has a kairos time for each of us. Let us patiently wait for it and make sure we don't miss it.

GOOD NIGHT, LORD

Lord, how often I have missed Your voice, missed Your direction, missed Your timing. Because of my own dullness of hearing, I have not been tuned to hear the voice of the Holy Spirit. Please forgive me. I want to start anew. I want to be so alert that I do not miss special times You have ordained for me, nor the special people You want me to know. I don't want to err on the other side either, hurrying things up which I think are of You. Waiting is so hard for me. Teach me how to do it with more sensitivity. I don't want to miss Your kairos time for my destiny. I ask this in Jesus' name. Amen.

Note
1. Ethelbert W. Bullinger, *A Critical Lexicon and Concordance to the English and Greek New Testament* (Grand Rapids, Mich.: Zondervan Publishing House, 1975), p. 804.

Aim on Target

Those who war with you will be as nothing, and non-existent.
For I am the LORD your God, who upholds your right hand,
who says to you, "Do not fear, I will help you."

ISAIAH 41:12,13, NASB

The Bible gives us several examples of courageous women who defended their spheres of influence. I especially like the courage of a certain unnamed woman in the Old Testament who literally saved her city, Thebez (see Judg. 9:50-57).

The wicked king Abimelech had ruled with terror for three years, killing 70 of his half-brothers. He had just destroyed a village of 1,000 people; his next target was to burn Thebez. When he came to the city, he and his men captured it, but there was a strong tower in the center where the men and women had shut themselves up on the roof. Then comes the story of our heroine.

Scripture says, "But a certain woman threw an upper millstone on Abimelech's head, crushing his skull" (Judg. 9:53, *NASB*). Then the wicked king told his armor bearer, "'Draw your sword and kill me, lest it be said of me, "A woman slew him."' So the young man pierced him through and he died" (Judg. 9:54, *NASB*).

Abimelech knew that only a woman would use the upper revolving millstone with a circular hole in it, because it was a domestic utensil used to grind grain—woman's work. A man would have attacked with a spear or bow and arrow, or another weapon of war.

This woman of Thebez had nothing to lose. She knew she'd be dead if she didn't do something, and so would her people. She used what was available to her—an upper millstone. Her aim was specific and on target. The results? The wicked king was killed, she lived, and her people were freed from terror. We could say she hit the bull's-eye.

It's interesting that the Hebrew root word for the word "intercessor" or "intercession" is *paga* (paw-GAH), meaning "to come between, to assail, to cause to entreat." When an Israeli soldier hits the mark in target practice, he shouts, "Paga!"—the modern Hebrew equivalent of "bull's-eye."[1] Effective prayer intercessors learn to hit the bull's-eye with accuracy in prayer warfare. They learn to see things from God's vantage point. They have come to know that the name of the Lord is their strong tower; they hide in Him and are safe (see Ps. 61:3; Prov. 18:10).

The woman of Thebez was in the right place at the right time to save her entire city. When I read her story, I am encouraged and strengthened to defend my own sphere of influence. Her example tells me that when the enemy comes to destroy what I hold dear, I have a weapon with which I can defend my bean patch: prayer. When I intercede for others by the Holy Spirit's direction and power, I am in the right strategic spot at the right time. When I align my prayers with what the Holy Spirit wants me to pray, I hit the bull's-eye. The same can be true of you. In whatever state you find yourself, you have a bean patch to bless, tend and defend.

GOOD NIGHT, LORD

Lord, when the enemy comes to destroy what I hold dear, enable me to use the spiritual weapons You've provided me. Help me to hit the bull's-eye in intercession. Though I don't know the name of the woman of Thebez, You do, and You know my name and every other woman who is calling out to You tonight on behalf of her loved ones. Thank You, Lord. Amen.

Note
1. Dutch Sheets, *Intercessory Prayer* (Ventura, Calif.: Regal Books, 1996), p. 99.

PART THREE

Experiencing
VICTORY DAYS

I see two things on the horizon: breakthrough in answered prayer—great victories to report—and an all-out assault of the enemy to wear down the saints and sabotage godly relationships. It's going to cost us to stand for righteousness. So if we know what to expect, we can avoid the enemy's tactics and gain victory through prayer.

Someone said, "We stop trying in trying times." Yet, persistence is the gold mine of success. Don't think of defeat as permanent, but as something that causes you to persist. There is nothing we need to persist in more than in praying for ourselves and others.

Two big hindrances to persistent prayer are unbelief and unforgiveness. Jesus told His disciples:

> Have faith in God. Truly I say to you, whoever says to this mountain, "Be taken up and cast into the sea," and does not doubt in his heart, but believes that what he says is going to happen, it shall be granted him.
>
> Therefore I say to you, all things for which you pray and ask, believe that you

have received them, and they shall be granted you.

And whenever you stand praying, forgive, if you have anything against anyone; so that your Father also who is in heaven may forgive you your transgressions (Mark 11:22-25, *NASB*).

When we are in right relationship with Jesus and have no unforgiveness and no unbelief, we can speak to our problems, obstacles, hindrances, circumstances—our mountain, whatever it may be. Through prayer we believe God is moving on our behalf . . . in His timing.

Wayne Meyers, long-time missionary to Mexico, had a saying that went to my heart concerning this Scripture. I have it posted above my desk:

Don't tell God how big your mountain is,
Tell the mountain how big your God is.

Right now, my prayer is to speak hope to every area of your hopelessness. Look around and see the victories God has brought about in your life as a result of your prayers. And if a specific victory is not yet on the horizon, do not stop asking God for a breakthrough. Trust Him that it will happen.

When Our Mountain Moved

Through God we shall do valiantly,
and it is He who will tread down our adversaries.

PSALM 60:12, NASB

As renewal swept America in the early 1970s, God touched our hearts; and my husband and I invited Him to help us establish a truly Christian home, though we had been teachers and officers in our denominational church for years. Our children, who had been in church with us since infancy, were in elementary school when we made an all-out commitment to Jesus as our Lord.

We started family devotional times around the kitchen table, instituted Bible memorization plans, encouraged our children to keep prayer journals and taught them to pray aloud, even as we were learning. I remember clearly the time each of our children stood publicly in a church and invited Jesus into their hearts.

Then came peer pressure, some rebellious years, days away at college when LeRoy and I really didn't know what was happening with them. This only drove us further into prayer. I spent hours digging through the Bible to find God's promises for us and our family. I asked the Holy Spirit to teach us.

LeRoy and I prayed together daily. We were forced to acknowledge that our enemy—God's enemy, Satan—was determined to keep our children in his camp. But we had God's promises and we stood on them.

After a five-year prayer battle, our children came back to God, each one in his or her own miraculous way. That didn't mean we could let down our guard. There were still many needs to cover in prayer for them—financial goals and struggles, health challenges, prayers for their mates and friends, career changes. And, of course, the godly wisdom they would need to raise their own children.

Sometimes we pray for a long time about a particular issue involving our loved ones, and then God answers our prayers in a sudden and surprising way. One such answer to a prayer of mine started on a cold Sunday morning. I was standing at the Western Wall in Jerusalem with my prayer partner Laura. Pilgrims come from all over to pray here—the only remains of the wall that once surrounded the temples built in the times of Solomon and Herod.

Just before we left our prayer watch, I pressed the names of my children into the cracks of the wall. Then I softly prayed one final prayer: "Lord, it is Your will to save. Give my children repentant hearts. Fulfill Your destiny in their lives."

Miracle of miracles! Before that day ended, back in Florida, the first of our three children had an encounter with the Lord. Here's how it happened: Sherry, a senior at Florida State University, was preparing to drive the 125 miles from our home back to campus. A blinding rainstorm delayed her trip, so she drove to the church her dad and I attended. After circling the building three times, she finally pulled into the parking lot and went inside.

A visiting pastor from Africa was there, speaking passionately on the verse "But seek first His kingdom and His righteousness; and all these things shall be added to you" (Matt. 6:33, NASB). He said emphatically, "God has a purpose for your life. Your job is to find out what it is and do it."

Sherry was touched deeply and began weeping as the Holy Spirit moved with conviction upon her heart. She was about to graduate and she was not sure what God's purpose was for her.

Steve—who was a student in Bible college in another town— was delayed by the storm, too, and he had also come to church.

He saw Sherry's tears and approached her gently but firmly. "Sherry, God's not putting up with you having one foot in the world and one foot in His Kingdom. You've got to make a choice. I hope it will be tonight."

She broke down and more tears gushed down her face. The battle was over. The Good Shepherd had found our lamb while we were in Israel and wooed her back through Steve, a longtime family friend.

The following weekend, back from our trip, we visited Sherry at her request and went to church with her. Sherry asked us to go to the altar and kneel with her. She asked our forgiveness for the years she had opposed God's plan for her life. We wrapped our arms about her and asked her to forgive us, too, for not being the parents we should have been and for failing her so often.

Sherry graduated from Florida State and enrolled in a Bible school in Dallas. Our other two, Quinett and Keith, came back to the Lord soon afterward—all within eight months of Sherry's return—and they followed her to Bible school.

The miracle to me is the way God chose to answer our prayers. Steve was one of the young men in the church for whom I had prayed on a regular basis. In fact, I kept a picture of him in my prayer journal, in my "bean patch" section. For eight long years I prayed for him every Friday while he served in missions in Greece, Germany and Israel and, later, while he was in Bible school.

What a valuable investment of my time and effort! For years, one of my prayers had been, "God, bring the friends of Your choice into my children's lives." That night, God did just that for Sherry. After years of praying, my sudden answer had come![1]

GOOD NIGHT, LORD

Thank You! You are such a faithful, loving God. There really is no moun-tain—no obstacle, circumstance, problem or hurdle too large for You and no person too far gone in rebellion against You that You cannot rescue in Your perfect timing. How truly grateful I am to You for moving our mountain and bringing our family back into rightful relationship with You. Thank You for those who stood in prayer with us and for those You used to speak truth in hard places. In Jesus' name I pray. Amen.

Note
   1. Quin Sherrer and Ruthanne Garlock, *How to Pray for Your Children* (Ventura, Calif.: Regal Books, 1998), pp. 65-68.

Roots and Heritage

I will pour out my Spirit on your offspring, and my blessing on your descendants.

ISAIAH 44:3

"Build on your roots and heritage," the sign said. I pondered that thought for quite a while. *Roots and heritage.* The words tumbled over and over in my mind, though I was not sure what they meant to me.

A few weeks later I found myself in the southern state where my dad grew up. I asked my friend Freda to drive me about an hour south. I wanted to visit my dad's gravesite for the first time. When he died, I was speaking in another country, and planes flew in and out of that location only twice a week. I knew he would have wanted me to stay and share the gospel, so I didn't attend his funeral.

Now we drove down asphalt backroads, passing fields dotted with blooming magnolia and dogwood trees—my favorites. The fragrance of jasmine blossoms reminded me of the ones running along my grandmother's front porch from so many years ago when my cousins and I slept out there on warm summer nights.

Finally, we saw a sign pointing to Sharon Cemetery, established in 1827. How would we find my dad's marker in this vast yard? By instinct I asked Freda to curve right and keep on driving. Then, near the entrance to Sharon Presbyterian Church, I spotted his tombstone with the dates June 9, 1910-May 1995. I got out of the car and walked around, trying to sort through my mixed emotions. Daddy had abandoned mother with four children when I, the oldest, was only 12. He married the other woman in his life and never got close to his children after that.

One night, when I was thirty-something, I chose to forgive my dad in a very emotional, life-changing experience while kneeling in a pastor's office. I chose to forgive Dad, not based on what I felt or what I wanted to do, but based on what God's Word required of me. Daddy was responsible for his own wrong-doing, but I was responsible for the resentment I'd held on to as a result of his desertion. I gave Jesus all my hate, bitterness and disappointment that night.

Then I started writing to Daddy, even inviting him to come see us. Five years later he did come for the first time ever, and he was alone. Some years later I had my second and final time alone with him. On that short half-day visit I drove him by the cemetery where we children had buried Mother.

"She forgave you long ago, Daddy," I told him.

"She was a good woman—worked hard for you children," he said. "By the way, I'm glad you forgave me, too."

I was too choked up to answer.

Now, as I walked about the cemetery, my eye was drawn to the grave of my beloved granddad buried on the other side of his son—my dad. Through the years, Granddad had given my mother encouragement and emotional support. Whenever he dropped in to see us, he had been my cheerleader—my father figure. "Girl," he would say, "you can do anything you set your mind to do if God is in it. He'll equip and help you."

As the thought crossed my mind that Granddaddy was part of my roots and heritage, too, I realized that I had never really been abandoned. I bowed my head in the silence of the cemetery and I began to pray, thanking God. I determined to uncover more of my spiritual genealogy and heritage handed down from my forefathers and mothers and felt excited to begin the treasure hunt.

GOOD NIGHT, LORD

Lord, thank You that You never abandoned me. You knew my destiny. You provided a grandaddy who came in and out of my life just when I needed a father figure. Then there was my dad. He passed on to me some of his genes—though not all his good ones, I'm sure. I thank You for his commendable capabilities, the talents and giftings his children inherited from him. At the cemetery I grew a bit sad thinking of all that he missed out on in life by his choice of staying away from us. He didn't get to know his 4 children well, let alone his 10 grandchildren. I know he had a relationship with You, Lord, and that he and my mother are both in heaven today. For that I am grateful. So I pause to thank You, Lord, for this man who was my dad. In Jesus' name. Amen.

Legacy of Love

Children's children are a crown to the aged,
and parents are the pride of their children.

PROVERBS 17:6

When my mother sold her boarding house in Tallahassee, she bought some rental cottages on the sound in the fishing village of Destin, Florida. My three children loved to visit her. They could dive off her dock or swim across to Holiday Island or go with her to the nearby Gulf of Mexico for a romp in the waves. They collected shells and cooked crabs and went fishing in the little pools all around her place.

But it wasn't all play. When work was involved, she made it fun, too, working alongside them. They learned how to book reservations for the cottages over the phone, how to rent them out and how to help her clean them after the guests checked out.

She taught my youngsters safety rules, expected obedience when she spoke and rewarded them with privileges that far outshone what we could have done for them. Grandchildren were to be enjoyed and loved, she said. When they came back home to us they talked nonstop about their adventures and admitted they shared some special secrets with her.

She'd sing with them, read to them, let them sit up late and study the stars. She'd even recite the "elocution" pieces she learned as a girl in high school—poetry and long essays she still remembered from the 1920s.

As my children grew older, they called her for prayer whenever they were facing a hard time—a test in school, a financial setback, a broken relationship—and she would pray with them right then on the phone.

Sometimes she would raise her hands to heaven during her prayer times and say, "Lord, these 10 fingers represent my 10 grandchildren. Now I bring them before Your throne to pray for them," and she'd pray specifically for each one daily.

She died a few weeks before my son graduated from college. At his graduation he looked heavenward and said, "How I wish Mother Jewett could have been here today to see me get this diploma. She helped me with her prayers." We all shed a few tears, remembering.

Wise grandparents leave a lifelong impression when they bestow love.

GOOD NIGHT, LORD

Lord, we thank You for grandparents who have spoken so lovingly into the lives of our children. Tonight I am particularly grateful for my mom—for what she imparted to my children through her sacrifice, love and wise counsel. I'm thankful, too, for the role model she was to me as a grandmother. Help me to be an even better grandmother to my five! Amen.

Give Children to God

Then Hannah prayed and said: "My heart rejoices in the LORD; in the LORD my horn is lifted high. My mouth boasts over my enemies, for I delight in your deliverance."

1 SAMUEL 2:1

Our pastor was conducting his own son's wedding service when he suddenly stopped and addressed the congregation, saying:

> This afternoon my wife and I brought all our children down to the church altar. As they knelt here, we literally gave all five back to God. His Word says that our children are a heritage from Him. I look on ours as gifts entrusted to us for just a while. Now our first child is leaving home, but he is dedicated to the Lord.

My pastor's words hit me like an arrow. Had I dedicated my children to God? When they were small, LeRoy and I had christened them in a church service. But should I do more now that I had grown in my Christian walk?

I started searching the Bible for Scriptures related to moms and children. One morning, a passage seemed to jump from the page into my heart. It was Hannah's surrender prayer to God for her little son, Samuel:

> I prayed for this child, and the LORD has granted me what I asked of him. So now I give him to the LORD. For his whole life he will be given over to the LORD (1 Sam. 1:27,28).

All day the words "So now I give him to the LORD" rang over and over in my heart. I realized that it didn't matter how old my children were; it was not too late to dedicate them to God—to release them to His loving plan and care. I chose to do that right then, speaking aloud to the Lord. I had a glorious prayer time as I gave them to God. Scary, yes, but I trusted God with their future.

Little could I know what lay ahead when my adult children made their decisions to live and travel for Jesus. One was gone for nine years, another for four years, still another for over a year—most of that time they were living at opposite ends of the globe. From Africa to Europe, from Asia to Israel, all three of my children tramped the continents for the Lord. Sometimes it was several years before one came home for a visit.

They had some close calls, some frightening experiences— like a bomb left on the doorstep of a daughter's apartment in Jerusalem. She also got caught smuggling Bibles into China but fortunately wasn't arrested. Eventually they all came home and settled close to us. They continue to serve the Lord in their homes and jobs.

I live a little over an hour from where the tragic massacre in Columbine High School in Littleton, Colorado, took the lives of 12 teenagers—8 of whom were professing Christians. One of those victims was a 17-year-old named Rachel. She had expressed a desire to be a missionary, to travel the world and let her light shine for Jesus. Instead, a fellow classmate gunned her down. Because her funeral was broadcast around the world and the gospel message was proclaimed without any interruptions, reports are still coming in of the hundreds of people—many of them youth—who have committed their lives to follow Jesus as the result of her death and sacrifice. "Rachel reached the entire world at her funeral—more than she could have reached in her lifetime," her pastor said.[1]

I often think of the reminder our pastor gave us at his son's wedding when he said that our children are gifts entrusted to us for just a short time. While we don't know what lies ahead for each of our children, we can put our trust in the One who does know. And we can rest assured that we will see them in heaven one day if they've made their decision to follow Jesus.

GOOD NIGHT, LORD

Lord, we don't know what You have planned for each of our children, but teach us to rest in the knowledge that You will carry it out in Your timing. Help us to prepare them spiritually and physically for their unique walk. And help us to release them—for each and every season of their lives. Keep them close to Your heart, Lord. Amen.

Note
1. Sermon at Abundant Life Worship Center, Nutley, N.J., June 1, 1999, by Pastor Bruce Porter of Celebration Christian Church, Littleton, Colorado.

My Promise Shell

"For I know the plans I have for you," declares the LORD, "plans to prosper you and not to harm you, plans to give you hope and a future. Then you will call upon me and come and pray to me, and I will listen to you. You will seek me and find me when you seek me with all your heart."

JEREMIAH 29:11-13

I clearly remember a day when the Lord spoke to me about my teenage son, Keith, as I walked the beach. Deeply concerned about his spiritual condition, I felt he was drifting further and further from the Lord. My only recourse was prayer.

I realized that as a parent, I had made so many mistakes. So I asked the Lord to forgive me.

That afternoon, as I walked alone, I proclaimed aloud Scriptures tucked away in my heart. "The seed of the righteous shall be delivered," I shouted into the wind. "Because of Jesus' blood I am righteous and my children are my seed and they shall be delivered," I paraphrased. "All my children shall be taught of the Lord, and great will be their peace," I paraphrased again. (See Prov. 11:21; Isa. 54:13, *KJV*.)

Over and over I repeated scriptural promises God had given me for my children. I desperately needed an answer for my son. After more than an hour of this, I reached down and picked up a small brown shell being tossed about by the waves. "Trust me to polish and perfect your son," the Lord seemed to whisper to my spirit as I turned the shell over in my hand.

I took my shell home, cleaned it and set it where I could see it whenever I cooked. "Lord, You promised," I would say some days as I cradled it in my palm. Even after Keith left for college and I saw little change, I thanked God for His word that He and He alone would perfect my son whom I loved so very much.

Our prayer battle ended one night when Keith called to ask his father and me to forgive him; we asked him to forgive us, too. He had started his pilgrimage back to the Lord. After college and a short career in graphic arts, he enrolled in Bible school.

Not long ago Keith finished seven years of service with the Youth With A Mission organization (YWAM). He's been twice to West Africa and to Indonesia, Thailand and parts of Europe as a short-term missionary. He has taught communication skills to staff onboard the hospital ship *Anastasia*, and he's had the privilege of training others to go to the nations for Jesus while teaching at the University of the Nations in Hawaii.

Today he's a godly husband to a wonderful wife and the father of two young daughters. My "promise shell" still sits in my kitchen, testimony to a prayer answer God gave me so many years ago.

When we ask, God often gives us a special assurance for our family. It may come from a Scripture verse we've tucked deep within our hearts or from something personal He whispers at an extraordinary moment. When we know we have heard from Him, we can stand on that word with sure faith until we see His promise actually fulfilled. We may have some hours—or years—of persistent prayer in store, but we must never give up. Nor must we give in to fear or guilt. God is faithful.

GOOD NIGHT, LORD

Lord, thank You for the way You have worked in the life of my son. For his love for You. For the way he is rearing his daughters to know You and call on You with their own childlike faith. Thank You that You were faithful to answer those prayers when I called out for him. Thank You for the wife You've sent him and their godly home. Lord, now that he's in the workaday world of graphic arts, I pray for his business to prosper, so he can take care of the financial needs of his family. Give him peace, wisdom, understanding, strength and ability to fulfill Your call upon his life. I ask this in Jesus' name. Amen.

Prodigals Come Home

*But we had to celebrate and be glad, because this brother of yours was dead
and is alive again; he was lost and is found.*

LUKE 15:32

Just as the famous prodigal in Jesus' parable came to his senses
and returned home after spending his inheritance on riotous living, today rebellious teens and young adults are also waking up
by the hundreds. Many young people who are addicted to drugs,
alcohol, sex or credit-card spending want to get free.

The biblical story of the prodigal holds an important lesson
for all parents, it seems to me. The father saw his son coming
from a long way off. He must have watched for him often—
maybe every day—with the hope and expectation that this was
the day he'd see the young man trudging toward home.

Remember the whole story? This "gimme" son had demanded his inheritance before it was due him. Then he blew it by
going to a distant country and spending his entire inheritance
on reckless living. When famine hit the land, he would have
gladly eaten the pods offered the hogs, but no one gave him anything. He knew his father's hired servants lived far better than he
did, so he came to his senses and headed home, willing to be just
a servant.

When the father spied his wayward son, he was so filled with
compassion that he ran to meet him and threw his arms around
him, kissing him over and over again. Parental love was show-
ered on him even before he admitted, "Father, I have sinned
against heaven and against you. I am no longer worthy to be
called your son" (Luke 15:21).

I believe the father had already forgiven this headstrong boy. Why? Because he immediately had his servants bring the best robe and put it on him. Then he gave his son a ring and sandals and threw a feast to celebrate his return. His father said, "For this son of mine was dead and is alive again; he was lost and is found" (Luke 15:24).

This was a Jewish boy, smelling from the pigpen. Yet his father's arms engulfed him and his heart welcomed him, giving his son the best he had.

As prodigals return home today, some are still stinking from the pigpen. Parents are required to make difficult decisions. Do they let them stay at home where they can get shelter, nutritious meals and love? Do they help with their rehabilitation? Hospitalization? Payment of debts? Do they take care of babies born out of wedlock?

Each family must make their own decision based on what God shows them for their individual situation. The rest of us must keep quiet and not make judgments outside our realm of authority or expertise. Our job is to pray and offer encouragement . . . and to forgive those in our own pigpen.

GOOD NIGHT, LORD

Thank You, Lord, that when we were outside Your perfect will for us, You wooed us to Yourself. We were all prodigals at sometime in our lives. Help us to forgive those who have wounded and hurt us and to welcome them back home without severe judgment or tongue-lashings. Help us to be more like the father in the prodigal son's story by showing compassion and by opening our arms and embracing those who come back into the fold. Amen.

Covenant-Keeping God

We will not hide them from their children; we will tell the next generation the
praiseworthy deeds of the LORD, his power, and the wonders he has done.

PSALM 78:4

I get excited every time I read the verse that says God keeps "his covenant of love to a thousand generations of those who love him and keep his commands" (Deut. 7:9). What an inheritance! And what a privilege to pass on to our children the greatest heritage possible—the example of our personal prayer lives, after which they can model their own.

I've watched my adult children almost outdistance me in prayer in recent years. Since becoming parents, they've learned the importance of praying earnestly for the little ones God has entrusted to them. Together, we—the grandparents and the parents—can teach these children to pray. For one thing, they hear us pray aloud for them often, in everyday situations, not just at the table or at bedtime. And they're catching on.

The other day, when Benjamin and his grandad Papa LeRoy were in our backyard playing softball, LeRoy injured his fingers trying to catch a high ball the three-year-old had whopped across the fence. Benjamin quickly grabbed his grandad's bruised hand and prayed, "Jesus, please heal his hurt. Amen."

Whenever I have the opportunity to hold one of our grandchildren in my lap, I say, "God has a plan and destiny for you. I call it forth in Jesus' name." They don't understand yet, but maybe someday they will remember as did Charles Spurgeon. One of the most noted British preachers of the nineteenth century, Spurgeon said his own conversion was the result of prayer—

the long, affectionate, earnest prayers of his parents, which he heard and God heard!

Through our prayers, our children and grandchildren can become powerhouses to change the world. We need believers in every field of work to reach others for Christ. Strengthened by the Holy Spirit and supported by our prayers, our offspring and their offspring can influence an ungodly world—revealing Christ to their fellow students, teachers or workmates—and be salt and light to their generation.[1]

GOOD NIGHT, LORD

Lord, bless the precious grandchildren You have given us. Help me to be a positive influence in their lives. Use them as Your ambassadors to win others to Christ. Thank You that You are a covenant-keeping God! I love You tonight, Lord, and am so grateful for the gift of children and grandchildren. Amen.

Note
1. Quin Sherrer and Ruthanne Garlock, *How to Pray for Your Children* (Ventura, Calif.: Regal Books, 1998), p. 219.

In an Instant

At that time men will see the Son of Man coming in clouds with great power and glory....If he comes suddenly, do not let him find you sleeping. What I say to you, I say to everyone: "Watch!"

MARK 13:26,36

Have you ever had your prayers answered suddenly, in an instant? Have you ever experienced a breakthrough, but you had to pinch yourself to believe that after all your prayers—sometimes over a period of years—suddenly the answer had come?

Betty called to tell me her brother had phoned her the previous night, announcing he had just accepted Jesus. The preacher told him to call someone who had been praying for him. Betty was having a hard time with the good news. "He's such a scoundrel," she remarked, "now on his fourth wife, after breaking up that family. How could God save him?"

I told her, "Remember the hours we prayed for him to repent and come to his senses? Thank the Lord he's now in the family of God."

Several days later, Betty was still shaking her head in disbelief. But I was rejoicing! My faith had been increased to believe the same could happen for some of my still wavering, wandering relatives.

There are many occurrences recorded in the Bible that build my faith. I call them "suddenlies."

- When it was time for Jesus to be born, suddenly the angels appeared to obscure shepherds in a field outside Bethlehem to tell them the blessed news (see Luke 2:9,13).

- When the day of Pentecost came, they were all together in one place. Suddenly a sound like the blowing of a violent wind came from heaven and filled the whole house where they were sitting (Acts 2:1,2).
- Saul, on the way to Damascus to persecute Christians, had a terrifying encounter leading to his conversion: "Suddenly a light from heaven flashed around him. He fell to the ground and heard a voice say to him, 'Saul, Saul, why do you persecute Me?'" It was Jesus Himself who gave him his life's assignment (see Acts 9:3-15). Saul became Paul and wrote a large portion of what we know today as the New Testament.
- Several times, God warned rebellious people that things would happened suddenly, in an instant (see Isa. 29:5; 30:13).
- The greatest "suddenly" this planet will ever experience will occur when Jesus Himself returns—a time that no man knows (see Mark 13:32).

God hears our prayers. Not one goes unheard. Scripture tells us that our prayers are stored in "golden bowls full of incense, which are the prayers of the saints" (Rev. 5:8).

Pastor Dutch Sheets writes, commenting on Revelation 8:3-5, "God has something in which He stores our prayers for use at the proper time. . . . either when He knows it is the right time to do something or when enough prayer has accumulated to get the job done, He releases power. He takes the bowls and mixes it with fire from the altar."[1]

Each of us can expect a "suddenly" if we are obedient to pray and then trust God for His answer.

GOOD NIGHT, LORD

Lord, I thank You for the times You suddenly answered a prayer of salvation—for my children, an aunt, a cousin. Thank You for the times You protected me, led me, even guarded me from wrong decisions. I knew in an instant I'd heard from You and made the right choice. I want to be more expectant for those sudden answers from You and not think they are just happenchance experiences. Amen.

Note
1. Dutch Sheets, *Intercessory Prayer* (Ventura, Calif.: Regal Books, 1996), pp. 208, 209.

You Are Him Here

And if anyone gives even a cup of cold water to one of these little ones because he is my disciple, I tell you the truth, he will certainly not lose his reward.

MATTHEW 10:42

That Sunday night, in an unplanned good-bye, the pastor let her address our congregation from the microphone. She was just 13.

"I've been here in the detention home for some months now," she admitted. "But on weekends I've been allowed to visit in some of your homes. You've fed me, clothed me and, best of all, you have introduced me to Jesus. I'm rehabilitated now and ready to return to my own town—my own home. But I'm so thrilled with what Jesus has done for me, I want to thank Him."

She raised a finger and pointed out at the audience. "While I want to thank Jesus, I remember that you are Him here, so I will thank you." There was hardly a dry eye in the sanctuary as she continued pointing her tiny finger at various ones who had exhibited the love of Jesus to her in practical ways.

Home. She was going home. That had two meanings now: a real home with parents and, someday, an eternal home with her heavenly Father.

After her public good-bye, our pastor had dozens of plaques made for any family in the church who wanted one. The plaque was inscribed with the words: "You are Him here." Many of us hung them in our homes as a reminder that we are Christ's representatives to anyone who enters our home.

Teresa of Avila, a sixteenth-century nun, wrote: "Christ has no hands on earth but yours. No feet on earth but yours, no eyes of compassion on earth but yours. He has no body on earth but yours."[1]

You are Him here!

GOOD NIGHT, LORD

Lord, help me to be a good disciple for You—a worthy representative. May our home also be a refuge where others will feel Your love and be ministered to in a way they will never forget. Amen.

Note
1. Veronica Zundel, *Eerdman's Book of Famous Prayers* (Grand Rapids, Mich.: Eerdmans, 1983), p. 51.

In Remembrance of Him

A man ought to examine himself before he eats of the bread and drinks of the cup. For anyone who eats and drinks without recognizing the body of the Lord eats and drinks judgment on himself.

1 CORINTHIANS 11:28,29

My friend's son has been confined in prison for a number of years. Few can grasp the depth of heartache she has suffered as a result. But her years of praying for him paid off when he came to know the Lord—even behind bars.

A few days before Easter he asked his mom and dad to join him for Easter sunrise service, though they were separated by several hundred miles and he was in solitary confinement. He was allowed no personal belongings except a Bible.

He saved some cereal that had no leaven in it and a bit of grape jelly that he mixed with water for grape juice. At daybreak he read from 1 Corinthians 11:24-26:

"This is my body, which is for you; do this in remembrance of me. . . . This cup is the new covenant in my blood; do this, whenever you drink it, in remembrance of me." For whenever you eat this bread and drink this cup, you proclaim the Lord's death until he comes.

As he partook of Holy Communion in his cell, he looked out through the bars on his window at the sun bursting through the early morning sky. Three doves flew by. To him they represented the Father, the Son and the Holy Spirit—a sign that God had not forgotten him.

He has repented of his sins and has become a new creature in Christ Jesus.

GOOD NIGHT, LORD

Lord, thank You that no sinner is too far gone for You to reach out and touch. Many mothers, like my friend, have children in jail or prison—some for robbery, rape, drug smuggling or kidnapping. Still others for murder or gang-related shootings. I pray that You give these moms hope that their offspring will also someday embrace Jesus as Savior. Comfort these moms tonight as You wrap Your arms of love about them.

Bring people to their children in prison who will lead them to Christ and disciple them. Bless the chaplains and prison ministry volunteers who go into these places. And thank You for the ways that we can remember and celebrate Christ's life, death and resurrection—especially in Holy Communion . . . no matter what our circumstances. I ask in Jesus' name. Amen.

Praying for a Dying Stranger

*But God, being rich in mercy, because of His great love with which He loved
us, even when we were dead in our transgressions, made us alive together with
Christ (by grace you have been saved), and raised us up with Him, and seated
us with Him in the heavenly places, in Christ Jesus.*

EPHESIANS 2:4-6, NASB

One of the reciprocal commands—"pray for one another"—
sometimes means getting involved with strangers. I remember a
day when my prayer partner Fran and I visited a critically ill
woman in a nearby military hospital. I didn't know her, but my
son had asked me to go because her son was one of his room-
mates.

"She's dying of throat cancer," my son told me, "and since
Mick has accepted the Lord, he wants to be sure his mother
knows Jesus, too, before she dies."

After Fran and I went into her hospital room, she told us she
had not been to church in years. Then she said, "I've turned my
back on God all these years . . . it's just too late."

"No, it isn't," we assured her. Then Fran led her in prayer to
ask God to forgive her and to accept Jesus as her Lord.

"Come live in my heart, Lord Jesus, I want to be yours," she
whispered. After that, I went to see her several times, taking her
a Bible and devotional helps. Soon she lost her voice and
couldn't talk. Within a few weeks she died.

At the funeral home, I met her son, Mick, and was able to tell
him, "She accepted Jesus before she died—I heard her whispered
prayer with my own ears. She was so happy you've become a
Christian."

I'd hardly finished telling Mick the good news when an older woman spoke up. "Forgive me for listening in, but I'm Mick's grandmother. I've prayed 40 years for my only daughter—my prodigal child—to come back to the Lord. She made it! She actually made it to heaven. Thank You, Lord. Thank You, Jesus."

I left the funeral home thanking God for the opportunity to be part of the answer to the prayers of that elderly mom. God wants us to pray for one another—sometimes even for strangers.[1]

GOOD NIGHT, LORD

Lord, I thank You for Your faithfulness in answering the prayers of a mother who cried out 40 long years for her prodigal daughter. Thank You that she had the privilege of knowing her prayers were answered and that her daughter would spend eternity with You. Thank You, too, for a son who prayed for his mom. Amen.

Note

1. From *How to Pray for Your Family and Friends,* © 1990 by Quin Sherrer and Ruthanne Garlock. Published by Servant Publications, Ann Arbor, Michigan, pp. 110, 111. Used by permission.

A Voice from the Past

Give thanks to the LORD, for he is good; his love endures forever.

PSALM 118:1

She called today—a friend I hadn't heard from in more than 20 years. She tracked me down through a friend of a friend because we had both moved since our last contact. Our 30-minute catch-up conversation seemed so short.

She wanted me to know how I had helped and encouraged her in her walk with God those many years ago. As she talked, I recalled how she, as an older woman in my life, had taught me such a valuable lesson when my children were still small. One day I asked her, "How can you make all five of your children feel so loved, so confident, so full of healthy self-esteem?"

"Each one thinks he or she is my favorite," she replied. "I think every child in the world wants to believe he is his mother's most beloved. I've always worked hard at spending quality time with each one of mine, so he or she feels special. I've tried to be genuinely interested in their activities, whether it was art, music, interior design or tennis. Still, I have to say, God is the One who gives me creative ways to be the mother each one of them needs."

She had helped me so much then, and she was still encouraging me today as she filled me in on her children and how faithful God had been in their lives.

GOOD NIGHT, LORD

Lord, continue to give us creative and positive ways to boost our children's self-esteem. They long to know that we are proud of them. How we must guard against trying to live our lives through our children. Lord, help us not to manipulate their choices of careers, friends or spouses by our selfish desires. Keep us sensitive to ways we can help them make right choices and decisions. Let them know our love and our pride in them and that they don't have to measure up to some unrealistic standard. And Lord, thank You for friends who encourage us along the way so that we can be better Christian parents. Bless my friend who called today. Amen.

Another Birthday

*I thought about the former days, the years of long ago; I remembered my songs
in the night. My heart mused and my spirit inquired.*

PSALM 77:5,6

Now that I've reached the golden years, I'm thankful for all my
past birthdays. Some women count wrinkles or gray hair. I count
my blessings. And I remember other birthdays with children or
friends gathered around me.

I especially remember my fortieth birthday with my best
friend, Lib, who also had her fortieth the same week. Our backyard barbeque, celebrating with mutual friends from church,
seems just days ago. Everyone wrote an ode, poem or letter to
give us, which was so personal and precious.

I think of other birthdays when our children were still at
home. All of us, except our son, have birthdays within a few days
of each other, so we usually had several days of celebration; and
we outdid ourselves in thinking up ways to surprise one another and make each celebration special for the birthday person.

Now that I have moved out West, no one here seems to know
when I reach another milestone—when I've made it through yet
another year. No traditions have been established, no long-term
friendships formed.

But every year when I go to the post office I can count on a
card from my friend Mary Jo back in Florida. She hasn't missed
a birthday in more than 25 years. Neither has Laura, 2,000 miles
away, who calls me long-distance. Or Fran or Lib or even my
Aunt Betty. They have never forgotten to send a "thinking of
you" remembrance.

It makes me want to be more sensitive to my new friends here,
to let them know their birthdays are special, too. And maybe, just

maybe, I'll start a birthday club so those of us "oldies" won't be forgotten on our day!

GOOD NIGHT, LORD

Lord, thank You for my health, my family, my friends, my home, my food and shelter. Lord, I never want to take these things for granted. Thank You for sustaining me through this past year. With every problem I've faced, Your wisdom has faithfully guided me. Whenever I felt weak, I could lean on Your strength. In the year ahead, please direct my path and help me reflect Your love to all around me. Thank You, Lord. Amen.[1]

Note

1. From *Prayers Women Pray*, © 1998 by Quin Sherrer and Ruthanne Garlock. Published by Servant Publications, Ann Arbor, Michigan, p. 29. Used with permission.

Who Are Your Friends?

A gossip separates close friends. . . . But there is a friend who sticks closer than a brother.

PROVERBS 16:28; 18:24

What names come to mind when you think of friends in the Bible who stuck closer than a brother? Moses had Aaron and Hur to hold up his hands during battle. David had Jonathan. Paul had Barnabas. Timothy had John Mark during his days of ministry. Jesus had Peter, James and John.

But what is a friend? Someone sent me a bookmark with this definition:

A friend is one who strengthens you with prayers
Blesses you with love
And encourages you with hope.
—Author unknown

In the novel *Anne of Green Gables* by Lucy M. Montgomery, Anne talks about dreaming all her life for a kindred spirit to whom she could confide her inmost soul.

I think every woman needs a bosom friend—more than one really—to whom she can tell her innermost needs, problems and concerns and know those burdens will not be shared with anyone else except the Lord in prayer.

It's been said that we become like our closest friends. Therefore, it can be a costly mistake to have a non-Christian or a weak Christian as a best friend. Of course we love the lost and reach out to them, but we need to remember that best friends influence the way we think and talk. I finally had to give up my best friend when I made an all-out commitment to follow Jesus. I laid that friendship at the Cross.

I've found that it's healthier to have several close friends to protect me from overdependence on one person. I prefer to have some best friends my own age and then some older friends who can coach me along life's way. I've also discovered that I'm motivated by different women at different seasons of my life.

Good, supportive friendships enjoy a special bond and hold each other accountable. Here's the type of best friend I look for:

- She brings out the best in me.
- She challenges me to grow in the Lord.
- She makes me laugh.
- She lovingly corrects me (in private).
- She helps me get my priorities straight.
- She encourages me when I'm down.
- She sees the best in me even on my unlovely days.
- She prays with me through tough times and good.

As I reflected on what my best friends have contributed to my life over the years, I'm grateful that:

- I learned a new depth of prayer from Fran.
- I learned to bake bread from Margaret.
- I learned to laugh from JoAnne.
- I learned to stretch food dollars from Lib.
- I learned to be hospitable from Johnnie, a pastor's wife.
- I learned from Mary Jo to decorate my home on what God had already provided.
- I learned to have a love for Israel after my oldest daughter, Quinett (one of my best friends), lived there several times and introduced us to Israeli traditions and decor.

I know that if I spend enough time with an acquaintance, she may eventually become a friend. So I always ask God to show me who I am to develop a close friendship with, and I do not stay boxed in to only those I call best friends right now.

GOOD NIGHT, LORD

I want to thank You tonight, dear Lord, for all the friends You have brought into my life over the years. Help me to be a better friend to those You want me to have closer relationships with during this particular season of my life. Keep me sensitive as I pray for them, encourage them and believe in them. Amen.

Prized Prayer Partners

Therefore confess your sins to each other and pray for each other so that you may be healed. The prayer of a righteous man is powerful and effective.

JAMES 5:16

Our private prayers are important and potent, but praying with a prayer partner helps strengthen our effectiveness.

Jesus encouraged us: "Again, I tell you that if two of you on earth agree about anything you ask for, it will be done for you by my Father in heaven. For where two or three come together in my name, there am I with them" (Matt. 18:19,20).

The word "agree" in this verse derives from a Greek word from which we get our English word "symphony." It means "to be in accord or in harmony" or "to make one mind."

Jesus was always in agreement with His heavenly Father. We, too, can ask the Lord for His mind about a situation or problem, then pray with a prayer partner in agreement—with one mind—until we see results.

For years I had two prized, dependable prayer partners. Lib was my age, with four children near the age of my three. We prayed every weekday morning by phone for five minutes, precisely at 8:00 A.M. When all seven of our children reached those challenging teen years, we were glad we'd started praying together when they were younger. Now we had more prayer ammunition with which to fight.

We learned new depths of prayer as we went through various crises with our youngsters—car wrecks, illnesses, emergency-room trips, minor brushes with the law.

Laura, at the other end of the scale, was my more mature-in-the-Lord prayer partner—five years ahead of me physically and spiritually. Though we lived 40 miles apart, we met twice a month to pray either at her home or mine. She was my encourager, my affirmer, my cheerleader.

"Hey, you're going to make it," she'd often say, laughing about a situation that looked hopeless to me. "Listen, one of my kids went through that pain. I'll help pray you through this. Believe me, it's not as gloomy as you think."[1]

Years later, when I moved, it took time to get knitted with the right "prayer support team." Finally, God put it together for six of us who focused our prayers on our families. We met at Fran's home at 5:30 each Monday morning for one hour. Then, as the others left to get children off to school or husbands to work, Fran and I spent another hour talking, praying and encouraging one another. We saw many miracles in our families during those three years of focused prayer. Not only did all of our children make new commitments to the Lord, but Fran's son was also healed of Hodgkin's disease when he'd been near death.

Today my husband is my best prayer partner, but not all women have husbands willing to pray daily with them. It's wise to ask the Lord for the right prayer support, no matter if it's one person or a team—people who will agree in prayer, in the way God has shown you to pray, until victory is accomplished.

GOOD NIGHT, LORD

Lord, I thank You for friends who are willing to share our prayer burdens, who are willing to stand in the gap until we see answers, no matter how long, and are willing to call and encourage and be there at a moment's notice. Thank You for the gift of friendships, especially with Christians who enrich our lives. I ask You to bless my husband for his faithfulness to take the time each day to pray with me over our family and neighborhood situations. For women who do not have this added support, I ask You to bring the right praying friends into their lives. I thank You for doing that. In Jesus' name. Amen.

Note

1. Quin Sherrer and Ruthanne Garlock, *How to Pray for Your Children* (Ventura, Calif.: Regal Books, 1998), pp. 66, 67.

The News Speaks

All who see them will acknowledge that they are a people the LORD has blessed.

ISAIAH 61:9

Sometimes God speaks through ordinary events. Maybe you think it's amazing or impossible that we can get a spiritual insight from reading the newspaper, but God can speak to us any way He wants, at any time, if we will only listen.

Not long ago, Ann Landers published a letter from a successful artist who said that when she attended her fiftieth class reunion, she learned that her high-school art teacher was still alive. She wrote a letter to that teacher, thanking her for her encouragment and for introducing her to art, which had greatly enriched her life. The teacher answered back, saying she was aware of her student's success, but in all the years she had taught, this was the first pupil to write and thank her.[1]

The Lord pierced my heart with that letter. How many people had I neglected to thank over the years? How many notes of appreciation had I sent to my mentors? To my spiritual moms? To pastors who had believed in me when I needed it most?

I stopped everything and wrote five letters of thanks that day, simply because I believe God spoke to me through a 250-word article in a newspaper.

I'd almost forgotten—had it been nearly 20 years?—that our pastor used to encourage us from the pulpit every once in a while to write a thank-you letter that week to just one person who had touched our lives. The letters I sent as a result of his challenge were written with love and deep appreciation. The ones I received were treasured and filed away to be read again.

In our everyday busyness we sometimes neglect to let those Very Important People we love know how powerfully we have been impacted by something they have said to us, done for us or given to us. We can take a lesson from the art student and her mentor.

GOOD NIGHT, LORD

Lord, I see Your love expressed so often in people who have been there for me—to encourage, love, correct and share. Thank You for the numerous people—friends and family alike—who have made such an impact on my life. I am richer and more blessed because they were a part of my training, discipline and growth. Bless them, Lord, for their willingness to get involved with me. Amen.

Note
1. Ann Landers, *Colorado Springs Gazette*, August 16, 1998, Life Section, p. 10.

A Stranger Blesses My Day

Practice hospitality to one another . . . [Be hospitable, be a lover of strangers,
with brotherly affection for the unknown guests, the foreigners, the poor, and
all others who come your way who are of Christ's body.]

1 PETER 4:9, AMP

"Would you put an Open for Business sign on your heart today? Don't be numb to other people's pain," the visiting preacher admonished our congregation.

For weeks his words stayed in my thoughts. *How could I have an open heart? What would that look like?*

God soon answered by questions by showing me a man sitting on a curb as I walked toward the door of my bank.

Just a poor homeless man, I thought to myself, glancing at him as I went into the bank to cash a check.

Give him some money, the Lord seemed to say.

"But, Lord, there are so many like him out in the streets—"

Do it for Me.

By the time I came outside again, he was still sitting on the curb, but now he was eating a hamburger. His Looking for Work sign was propped up against him.

"The Lord Jesus wants you to have this," I said, pushing a few bills into his hand.

"Well, isn't that just like our wonderful Jesus? I only met Him for the first time last week. He has been so kind to me. See this hamburger? A lady just brought it to me from McDonald's. Won't you sit down and share it with me?"

I smiled. A homeless, hungry man, offering me a part of his hamburger—maybe the only meal he would eat that day.

"Thank you very much, but lunch is waiting for me at home," I told him. Back in the car I thanked the Lord that He had allowed me to meet one so recently born into His kingdom. A brand-new believer with no biblical training, yet already he was demonstrating hospitality, willing to share with another.

GOOD NIGHT, LORD

Thank You, Lord, for this wonderful encounter today, for the way You speak to us and lead us. I would have missed a blessing myself had I not gone to talk to the man with the smile. Help me to keep my heart open for business—Your business. Amen.

Applying the Blood

Since we have confidence to enter the Most Holy Place by the blood of Jesus, by a new and living way opened for us through the curtain, that is, his body, . . . let us draw near to God with a sincere heart in full assurance of faith. . . . Let us hold unswervingly to the hope we profess, for he who promised is faithful.

HEBREWS 10:19,20,22,23

To apply the blood of Jesus over ourselves and our loved ones in prayer and spiritual warfare is one way to declare to the devil that Christ's blood creates a boundary that he cannot violate.

Only believers who have accepted—or appropriated—Christ's sacrifice for their sins can apply this precious blood. But we must not treat this as some magic formula that guarantees protection from adversity.

The practice of applying the blood is based upon the account in Exodus 12 of the first Passover. God instructed the Israelites to kill an unblemished lamb and place the blood upon the doorposts and lintels of their homes to protect their firstborn from the death angel. The angel "passed over" the homes with the blood but took the lives of every firstborn Egyptian. That lamb was a foreshadowing of the Lamb of God, Jesus Christ—our sacrificial lamb.

My friend Lucy used this prayer weapon during a recent violent thunderstorm when winds whipped about their home at hurricane force. She told me:

> I started pleading a "blood line" all around our farm and around my son's farm across the road—and over every one of our buildings, fields of crops, machinery, trailer house, the cattle, the horses, even the huge pine trees. Then I laid my hand on my Bible and repeated the plead-

ing of the blood line around all our property. The storm hit with full force, rain came in torrents, fast and powerful, as did hail. In the midst of the storm, I praised God over and over. When it was over our property was completely unscathed. Not even the patio furniture cushions had moved an inch. Our home and our son's are safe. Thanks and praise be to our God.

Who hasn't sung these words from the wonderful old hymn by Lewis E. Jones?

Would you over evil a victory win?
There's wonderful power in the blood.
There is power, power, wonder-working power in the blood of the Lamb![1]

The blood of Jesus is the basis of our authority over the enemy. Praise God for that!

GOOD NIGHT, LORD

Father, we thank You for the power in the blood of Jesus. Let us never take for granted what He did at Calvary for us. Amen.

Note
1. Lewis E. Jones, "There Is Power in the Blood," 1927.

Forgiveness Is a Choice

Get rid of all bitterness, rage and anger, brawling and slander, along with
every form of malice. Be kind and compassionate to one another, forgiving
each other, just as in Christ God forgave you.

EPHESIANS 4:31,32

Forgiveness, I've discovered, is not a one-time choice. It's ongoing and progressive. It is not an emotion; it is an act of the will—a choice, a decision, a demonstration of love. I may forgive without feeling an emotion. My part is to forgive; God's part is to heal.

The apostle Paul said he forgave "in order that Satan might not outwit us. For we are not unaware of his schemes" (2 Cor. 2:11). One of the enemy's schemes, then, is to keep us in unforgiveness. We have to choose to forgive so that Satan won't have a legal claim to oppress and torment us—to keep us in bondage.

Jesus said, "Forgive, and you will be forgiven" (Luke 6:37). Forgiveness means "to release, set at liberty, to release as unchaining someone."

When we don't forgive, we are binding ourselves to that person or situation and to the pain, emotional hurt and consequence it brings. "But you don't know what he did to me," you may be saying. No, I don't. Nor do you know what I had to let go of through unforgiveness. Painful, awful hurts!

A woman who was abused by her father decided that when she became an adult and asked Christ to take charge of her life, she had to forgive him. She memorized many Scriptures and spent hours praying for her father. One day, she prayed: "Heavenly Father, I choose to forgive my earthly father. If he had

had his mind trained on You, he would not have done what he did to me. I do not hold him responsible. Bring him to a right, godly state of mind."

Fortunately, her father turned to the Lord and became a Christian. But not all the people we forgive will have such a heart-change.

When we forgive, it doesn't mean our aggressor gets off free. It means we are unchained, loosed; we have given up our desire to get even. Once, we were both in prison; now we are free.

GOOD NIGHT, LORD

Lord, I'm so grateful that when I choose to forgive, You provide the grace I need to see me through the process. It is so hard at times, especially when the person continues to hurt and slander. Help me to forget as well as forgive. Sometimes it feels like I'm nursing a busted toe. I know it's healing, but when someone stomps on it, it hurts and bleeds again. Enable me to forgive as Jesus did on the cross. Amen.

Taken for Granted

O beautiful for spacious skies,
For amber waves of grain,
For purple mountain majesties
Above the fruited plain!
America! America!
God shed His grace on thee,
And crown thy good with brotherhood
From sea to shining sea!
—Katherine Lee Bates, "America, the Beautiful"

More than 100 years ago, after Katherine Lee Bates ascended to the top of Colorado Spring's Pike's Peak (14,110 feet high), she wrote the song "America, the Beautiful," which is sometimes called "O Beautiful for Spacious Skies."

From my home-office window, I have a commanding view of Pike's Peak. When the weather is warm enough, I find myself going out on our deck with hymnbook in hand and, as I face Pike's Peak, I read as a prayer all four verses of this song about our homeland. I especially like "America! America! May God thy gold refine."

I admit I used to ignore the good points of this place where I now live and concentrated instead on the negatives. The high altitude affects my breathing. I would grumble about the icy streets, high winds, hailstorms and piles of snow to be shoveled out of the driveway. I absolutely disregarded the beauty of Pike's Peak that God had set before me.

All along God was trying to refine me into gold, but I was not cooperating. I didn't appreciate where I was at the moment—at that season of my life—by His design.

A friend who was visiting me said, "You should thank God every day for the beauty of this place. Take time to audibly thank Him for something your eyes can see."

This statement jolted me back to seeing God's beauty displayed around me in His earth. Now I often find myself thanking God aloud for brilliant rainbows, dazzling golden aspen trees, clear and cool mountain waterfalls and yes, even a beautiful overnight snowfall.

GOOD NIGHT, LORD

Lord, how easy it is to take for granted where I live. Help me to develop an attitude of gratitude for our beautiful earth and for my city, state and nation. Thank You that You knew where I need to live. You've called me to pray for the welfare and peace of the city where You've planted me. Thank You, Lord. Amen. (See Ps. 24; Jer. 29:7.)

People or Things?

The LORD bless you and keep you; the LORD make his face shine upon you and be gracious to you; the LORD turn his face toward you and give you peace.

NUMBERS 6:24-26

I was participating in an overseas outreach mission with 15 other women in an Indian village high in the Guatemalan mountains. After distributing medicine, clothes, gospel messages and love to the people who had come to the rustic church, we began hiking ever higher up the mountain through cornfields, past coffee trees, going still higher until we could almost touch the clouds as they rolled in about us.

We had brought clothes for the pastors and their children, but one pastor asked that we come and pronounce a blessing on his home. Hence our need to climb to his residence—a modest one-room shanty with a simple tin roof and a dirt floor where baby chicks scratched at our feet. The entire family lived in the one room!

Suddenly my eye was drawn to wildflowers peeking out of a rusty tin can. The pastor's wife had placed a touch of beauty to turn her modest house into a home. Truly we felt the presence of the Lord as we praised God with songs in three different languages.

As I edged my way down the mountain to the flatbed truck that would transport us back to the village, I began to reflect on the peace and tranquility I'd experienced in that tiny house. I was reminded of a recent experience in the enormous home of a relative a few weeks earlier. After emerging from their swimming pool, I had accidentally gotten a few drops of water on his hardwood floors. I'd been admonished for the deed—didn't I know they were imported and expensive? Embarrassed and truly sorry,

I apologized. Then I said, "Do you care more about people or things?" He just shrugged his shoulders without answering.

Now, as I reflected on these two Christian homes in diverse settings, I was struck with the contrast. Where did I feel Christ's presence more? In the Indian woman's hut, where a kerosene lantern and her cookstove lit with sticks of wood she'd gathered provided the only source of light. Jesus, the Light of the world, was reflected there.

GOOD NIGHT, LORD

Oh, Lord, as I examine my own heart, I know I am often prone to put things before people. Please forgive me. Let my life and my home reflect Your love. Help me to be careful when I'm visiting someone else's home— to treat with care the things they hold precious and valuable. Thank You that when I ask Your forgiveness You freely give it. Amen.

A Dream Fulfilled

For God does speak—now one way, now another—though man may not per-
ceive it. In a dream, in a vision of the night, when deep sleep falls on men as
they slumber in their beds, he may speak in their ears.

JOB 33:14-16

Once a year my friend DeDee[1] and I attended a board of directors'
meeting for a ministry we were involved in on the West Coast.

One winter, while there for three weeks of meetings, DeDee,
an African-American, made her first appointment in a village
beauty salon. A young white man shampooed and styled her
hair.

As they talked, he told her he had five children; the eldest
was 10 years old. He was having a hard time getting them to
obey. Out of desperation, he had started attending a church. But
he admitted to DeDee that he was truly uninformed about biblical principles to use in rearing his family. DeDee suggested that
if he read the Bible he'd be more familiar with God's guidelines
for fathers. She encouraged him to raise his children with a
Christian heritage.

"I can't always understand the Bible," he told her. "I will try,
though."

As she walked out of the shop after her second visit, she
clearly heard God's voice: "Go buy him a Bible."

A friend drove her to a Christian bookstore. There she
prayed over the variety of Bible translations on the shelf, asking
God which one to buy. Finally, she chose one written in modern
English. It included a plan that showed him how he could read
through the Bible in one year by reading just 10 minutes a day.

The next afternoon, she walked down to the beauty shop
and handed him a bag, saying, "I have a present for you."

He didn't open the bag immediately. Instead he said, "Step outside a minute, will you? I have something very important to tell you."

Once outside he looked in the bag and to his surprise and delight, he pulled out the beautiful Bible. Tears glistened in his eyes. "I didn't know if I would ever see you again. I knew you didn't live here. But I have to tell you this. I was raised in the Catholic church. One night when I was just 16, I had a dream that a black nun would someday come and talk to me about the Lord. She was wearing a green winter coat and hat—dressed exactly like you. I realized after you left last time that you were the woman in my dream. But now it really falls into place—because the black woman also brought me a Bible."

"God wanted you to have this Bible," DeDee said. "Now you will know the Word of God and can explain it to your children."

"I will read it," he assured her, hugging the Bible to his chest.

A 16-year-old boy had a dream that came to pass 13 years later because a woman who lived 2,000 miles away came across his path, heard God's voice and obeyed.[2]

GOOD NIGHT, LORD

Lord, thank You for the various ways You still speak to us. When DeDee came back from delivering the Bible, her smile reflected the joy that comes when we hear Your instructions and then obey. I'm glad that young man will read the Bible she gave him and instruct his children in the ways of the Lord, because it was You who gave him the dream years ago about a messenger dressed just like DeDee who would come to deliver it. How awesome are Your ways! Amen.

Notes

1. Not her real name.
2. From *Listen, God Is Speaking to You*, © 1999 by Quin Sherrer. Published by Servant Publications, Ann Arbor, Michigan, pp. 152-154. Used by permission.

How to Reach Them?

Now to the King eternal, immortal, invisible, to God who alone is wise, be honor and glory forever and ever. Amen.

1 TIMOTHY 1:17, NKJV

My friend Hilda and her husband raised their four children during the 1960s when hippies smoking marijuana and flower children attending rock concerts seemed to be the norm. Though their children had attended church since they were young, as teenagers their behavior reflected the influence of peer pressure. What heartache Hilda endured when one son was in jail instead of marching down the aisle to receive his high-school diploma.

One by one her children left home to careers, college, marriages. All the while Hilda prayed for them to return to their Christian roots.

One year, when all four children—now adult and married—were visiting for Christmas, Hilda told them the only gift she wanted was one hour of their undivided attention. They agreed.

She set up her Sunday School flannelboard in her dining room. As they watched, she moved the characters and scenery, taking them on a Genesis-to-Revelation tour through the Bible, emphasizing Jesus' death on the Cross for their sins. Captivated by her lesson, they sat at the dining table for two more hours, asking their mom questions.

The Holy Spirit began wooing them and their spouses, and one by one over the next few months, they all committed their lives to the Lord. Today they are rearing their children in Christian homes and teaching them from the Bible, too.

In telling me about that turnaround day when she became teacher instead of just Mom, Hilda explained: "The enemy had ensnared all my children, and I knew I had to fight for each of them. It wasn't an easy battle. But knowing that it wasn't God's will for any of them to be lost, I persisted in using Scripture verses of God's promises to me. I often told Satan my children were God's property and he had to take his hands off them!"

And he did! Hilda's adult children are such a joy, not only to their parents but to others who share their lives.

GOOD NIGHT, LORD

Lord, how I thank You for Hilda's persistent prayer and for bringing her children back to You. You are indeed a God who restores. Thank You for sending her into my life at a time when I needed assurance for my own children who weren't exactly walking with the Lord. Tonight I want to thank You—for You are an awesome God. Amen.

One Mother's Idea

Again , I tell you that if two of you on earth agree about anything you ask for,
it will be done for you by my Father in heaven. For where two or three come
together in my name, there am I with them.

MATTHEW 18:19,20

What can one mom possibly do to halt the confusion or destruction that often accompanies the after-high-school graduation ceremony?

Concentrated prayer, that's what.

Only 37 students were scheduled to graduate from the tiny rural school, but Shiela, along with other concerned parents, decided they didn't want any wild drinking parties or car accidents—there had been far too many in recent years.

For three weeks before the end of the school term, Shiela opened her home for prayer. Any parent of a graduating senior was invited to come. Usually, at least four parents came and prayed together following this pattern:

- They prayed for each student by name, asking God to bless each one as he or she graduated, sought a job or went off to college.
- They prayed there would be no deaths or serious accidents resulting from drinking and driving.
- They prayed against the confusion that often accompanies the awards part of the commencement service—whistling, screaming or yelling during the ceremonies. (This year they wanted none of that disrespect.)

All these prayers were answered. There were no incidents at commencement exercises or in the celebration afterward to mar this special time for the young people and their families. Convinced of the power of praying in agreement, these parents planned another prayer session for the next year's graduates.

GOOD NIGHT, LORD

Lord, when this mother shared with me her God-inspired idea, I was excited that You had truly answered the prayers of these concerned praying parents. In a way I felt guilty that I hadn't thought of it for my own youngsters. But guilt and regret accomplish nothing. May other parents stand in the gap for their youngsters at such special times in their lives. Amen.

God's Embroidery

But thanks be to God! He gives us the victory through our Lord Jesus Christ.
Therefore, my dear brothers, stand firm. Let nothing move you. Always give
yourselves fully to the work of the Lord, because you know that your labor in
the Lord is not in vain.

1 CORINTHIANS 15:57,58

When Dutch evangelist Corrie ten Boom taught, she often used a poem about a piece of embroidery.

While displaying a portion of needlework, she would say, "God knows what we do not know. God knows all. Look at this piece of embroidery. The wrong side is chaos. But look at the beautiful picture on the other side—the right side." Then she would repeat this poem:

The Weaver
My life is but a weaving, between my Lord and me,
I cannot choose the colors, He weaveth steadily.
Ofttimes He weaveth sorrow, and I in foolish pride
Forget He sees the upper, and I, the underside.
Not 'til the loom is silent and the shuttles cease to fly,
Shall God unroll the canvas and explain the reason why.
The dark threads are as needful in the skilled Weaver's
    hand
As the threads of gold and silver in the pattern He has
    planned.
—Author unknown

"We see now the wrong side," she would add. "God sees His side all the time. One day we shall see the embroidery from His side and thank Him for every answered and unanswered prayer.

The joyful thing is that all the time we have to fight the fight of faith, God sees His side of the embroidery. God has no problems concerning our lives—only plans. There is no panic in heaven."[1]

Corrie was born in Holland in 1892. She died April 15, 1983, on her ninety-first birthday. She and family members had been imprisoned by the Nazis for using their home as a hiding place for Jews during World War II. She knew firsthand the suffering of being in prison and of losing both her father and sister due to the harsh treatment there. Yet she learned to forgive those who imprisoned her. Later, as she traveled the world speaking, she called herself a tramp for the Lord.

My friends Fran and Mike often hosted Corrie in their home. It was a place she could rest and work, and she wrote many of her books there. At her request, when she died one of her framed embroidery pieces was sent to them: Jesus Is Victor, it declares in brightly colored threads. Whenever I stay overnight with them, I request Corrie's bedroom, where I can enjoy looking at small keepsakes from her life that are on the dresser or displayed on the walls.

My favorite of all Corrie momentos is the framed Jesus Is Victor tapestry in their dining room, which Corrie created from design to finish. It is like a sentinel drawing us to the lesson of the poem Corrie made famous about the Weaver. Yes, God sees His plan all along, even when we don't.

GOOD NIGHT, LORD

Lord, thank You for the lessons so many of Your saints gave us by the way they lived. Though it was so long ago, it's as if I can still hear Corrie say, "Jesus Was Victor, Jesus Is Victor, Jesus Will Be Victor." Sometimes, when I think You aren't listening to my prayer pleas, I am reminded that You know better than I what Your final design is for my life. Help me to flow with what You want and remember that though I may see the ugly side of the design, You see the beautiful side. Amen.

Note

1. Corrie ten Boom, *Not Good If Detached* (London: Christian Literature Crusade, 1957), pp. 95, 96.

Leaving a
Prayer Legacy

Only be careful, and watch yourselves closely so that you do not forget the things your eyes have seen or let them slip from your heart as long as you live. Teach them to your children and to their children after them.

Laura came across a letter her Uncle Ted, a missionary, had written to his mother on her eighty-first birthday:

> Thank God that our every memory of you is one of beauty and holy living and rare parental guidance. Every one of us will be able to remember our family prayers morning and night. And how you taught us the Scriptures. We thank God for such a wonderful, God-fearing, praying and loving mother.

Laura's grandmother went to heaven just three months after receiving that letter. But her prayers and the influence of her godly life are still an active blessing for her children, grandchildren and great-grandchildren. Following a family reunion several years ago, Laura realized that all her grandmother's descendants were Christians.

What a heritage to ponder! What a tradition for all mothers (and all of us) to follow: to pray for our children (and others in our extended family) and *with* our children—and to live godly lives before them. The results are always far-reaching. Heaven will be full of the evidence.[1]

Just a few years ago, I attended a memorial service for a beloved pastor—a service I will never forget. During the service, his widow, their five children, their spouses and all their grand-children gathered on the church's platform. The moment had come to dedicate the newest baby, the thirteenth grandchild, to the Lord.

The words of the officiating pastor still ring in my ears: "Moses is dead, but Joshua will inherit the promised land." Joshua was the name of the grandson being dedicated to God—at his grandfather's funeral. Tears spilled down my face at this awesome occasion.

His last will and testament was read, recounting the Christian heritage passed to him from his parents; then it described his own walk with the Lord during his 60 years of life. He challenged his children and grandchildren to continue passing on this spiritual heritage from generation to generation. I listened, enthralled. I could just imagine how his children and grandchildren felt, even as they were saying their good-byes to the family patriarch. He was already in heaven with his Lord, they were assured. They had a choice to follow, too.[2]

GOOD NIGHT, LORD

Lord, how I long to follow the example of Laura's grandmother. May I be faithful in praying for my family and extended family. Someone said we don't take anything to heaven but those people we have introduced to Jesus. Lord, I want to see all of my family enjoy eternal life with You. Thank You for real-life illustrations from others' lives to inspire and challenge us. Amen.

Notes
1. Quin Sherrer and Laura Watson, *A Christian Woman's Guide to Hospitality* (Ann Arbor, Mich.: Servant Publications, 1993), p. 103.
2. Quin Sherrer and Ruthanne Garlock, *How to Pray for Your Children* (Ventura, Calif.: Regal Books, 1998), p. 106.

He Is Not Here

But the Comforter (Counselor, Helper, Intercessor, Advocate, Strengthener, Standby), the Holy Spirit, Whom the Father will send in My name [in My place, to represent Me and act on My behalf], He will teach you all things.

JOHN 14:26, AMP

It was a day after Christmas many years ago when I made my first trip to Israel. Security was extremely tight because of recent wars. We were searched meticulously.

At daybreak on an extremely cold morning, our group gathered in a beautifully manicured garden spot outside the main gates of Jerusalem. An open tomb was before us, possibly the one that once held the body of our Lord Jesus. We were here at the Garden Tomb to celebrate His resurrection.

After we sang about His rising from the tomb, a pastor delivered a short message. "Remember how you were searched before you came into Israel?" he asked.

Did I remember! I was one of few who was given a "body search"—thorough and embarrassing.

"You smuggled something into Jerusalem they couldn't take away from you in customs. It's not found in museums or in any of the historical places."

What was he getting at?

"You smuggled Jesus into Jerusalem! They couldn't lock that up. If you know Him, then His Spirit lives within you. The Bible says it is 'Christ in you, the hope of glory.'" (See Col. 1:27.)

Those of us on this Christian pilgrimage had brought the Spirit of the Living Lord into Israel with us. Like the women at the first resurrection, we could say, "He is not here. He is risen as He said."

GOOD NIGHT, LORD

Father, Thank You that after Jesus returned to heaven, He sent, as He promised, the sweet Holy Spirit to indwell us. Lord, don't let me take that gift for granted. Help me to yield more and more to what You want to accomplish in me and through me. In the name of Your Son, Jesus, I pray. Amen.

No Bread from Stone

The Jews began to grumble about him because he said, "I am the bread that came down from heaven. . . . No one can come to me unless the Father who sent me draws him, and I will raise him up at the last day."

JOHN 6:41,44

I shaded my eyes with my hands to get a better view of the wrinkled hills strewn with boulders. I had never pictured the Judean wastelands as littered with blistered, jagged rock. Nor had I imagined them to be so bare, devoid of greenery. Even in January the desert reflected sweltering heat. Quite a contrast to the cold, windy streets we had left behind in Jerusalem.

As we walked along, I tried to imagine what it was like when Jesus traveled this route from Jerusalem to Jericho. Near here He faced temptations that could have threatened His entire ministry.

My foot hit a rock, a warm stone about the size of a loaf of bread. As I picked it up, I remembered the account in the Gospel of Matthew of Jesus being led by the Spirit into the wilderness to be tempted by the devil. After He had fasted 40 days, the tempter told Him, "If you are the Son of God, command these stones to become loaves of bread."

Hungry. Alone. Exhausted. Hot. Turn stones to bread? Of course He could. He was the Son of God. But He didn't have to prove it to the evil one. Instead, Jesus replied, "It is written, 'Man does not live on bread alone, but on every word that comes from the mouth of God'" (Matt. 4:4).

Later, Jesus was to declare to His followers that He was the Bread of Life. "He who comes to me will never go hungry, and he who believes in me will never be thirsty" (John 6:35).

In Jesus' day bread was a staple, the most important food they ate. It was a symbol of God's gift of seed and harvest of grain. It was never wasted, and even inedible bread was softened with water to feed the birds.

The last meal Jesus would eat with His disciples would be the breaking of bread to observe the Lord's Supper.

There in the wilderness Jesus could have turned the stony loaves into bread or performed a thousand other miracles on the spot to prove His divinity. But there was no need.

Three short years later, after an abbreviated earthly ministry, He gave His body as the supreme sacrifice, dying so that we might live eternally.

The rock in my hand was heavy, so I let it fall to the ground. I selected a smaller, more rounded stone instead.

Back home on the first cool day of February, I put my hand into the pocket of my green coat. Still resting there was the little pebble I had picked up in the Judean wilderness, a reminder of a stone that could have been turned into bread by the Son of God—the Christ who still lives and is the Bread of Life.

GOOD NIGHT, LORD

Lord, how I thank You for the example You set in not giving into temptation when You were so hungry there in the wilderness. Help me to resist temptation, to take a stand against the devil's schemes. Sometimes it is difficult not to give in when I'm hurt or offended or treated badly. While I know that my wrong reaction can be expensive, help truth become more real to me. I desire to live a life pleasing to You. But I can't do it without Your help. Amen.

Please Pray with Me

So then you are no longer strangers and aliens, but you are fellow citizens with the saints, and are of God's household, having been built upon . . . Christ Jesus Himself . . . the corner stone.

EPHESIANS 2:19, 20, NASB

I was sitting in an aisle seat of the airplane when the flight attendant knelt beside me and whispered, "If I come back later, will you pray for me?"

"Sure, I will," I said. "But how do you know I'm a Christian?"

"There's a man in the back of the plane reading a book about prayer. He said you wrote it and gave it to him while you were waiting to board."

She returned to my seat later and knelt again to whisper of some desperate marriage struggles. I prayed with her right then, asking God to give her wisdom, discernment and strength. She cried, wiped her eyes then got up off her knees and patted my hand, flashing me a smile.

Sometimes God sends people into our lives by His divine appointment. Often I've missed those opportunities because I didn't want to be bothered.

My friend Barbara prays that God will order things in her life during her week—everything down to the smallest detail. "Every contact, every conversation, every point of communication—according to His divine purpose," she says.

One week she prayed this before attending a Christian conference where she knew no one. She had a two-minute prayer encounter with a woman she stopped to talk to on the sidewalk there. Five years later that woman opened doors of ministry opportunity for Barbara and, in the process, they became long-time friends.

Barbara told me, "Imagine . . . all along God knew! He kept track. He fulfilled His holy purpose—an appointed time, place, person and ministry. God not only gave me the two minutes with Dot, He watched over our prayers until the season for their fullness."

To us it may seem strange to pray aloud, especially with a stranger. But if God gives you that urge, He'll also give you the boldness and the Holy Spirit's guidance in how to pray.

GOOD NIGHT, LORD

Lord, don't let me be too busy with my agenda that I miss Yours. I give You permission to send the people of Your choice into my life—anytime. Maybe some of those strangers will turn out to be friends. And when I pray for them, let it be a God-inspired prayer. Amen.

Dream House

So we, who are many, are one body in Christ, and individually members one of another. And since we have gifts that differ according to the grace given to us, let each exercise them accordingly.

ROMANS 12:5,6, NASB

"Say, your living room really has potential. If you rearranged the furniture you could accommodate more people for all your Bible studies here." The woman speaking was Mary Jo, a grandmother whom I'd only met one other time but who had shown up for my writing class that night.

She offered to bring some friends from her church over to give our whole house a facelift. Her stipulation: my husband had to agree. With LeRoy's consent I invited her.

But first I called her pastor to check out her credentials. Though she had no professional training as an interior decorator, she had a God-given gift. He had let her redo both his home and office. Mary Jo had a team of women who accompanied her. Some did the sewing (curtains, bedspreads, tablecloths), some flower arrangements, some the moving of furniture, while others rearranged the wall hangings.

"God has already supplied what you need to decorate—it's just hidden in your closets, attic, garage or under your bed," she warned me in advance. Not wanting her to look in those "hidden" places, I pulled out things I thought she might use for decoration and stashed them on my patio table. I even unpacked some glassware of my grandmother's.

On Thursday morning when Mary Jo showed up with her friends, I can tell you I was plenty concerned. *Was I crazy to invite complete strangers to redo our house?* My fears eased after they sat on the couch and prayed: "Lord, may Your creative gifts flow through each of us so that we will decorate this home to Your glory, yet reflect the personality of the family who lives here. Holy Spirit come and use us as instruments with our varied talents."

I thought she would start with the living room. But instead she marched us all upstairs to the master bedroom. "Since this is the sanctuary for you and your husband, we'll start here. Go down to your living room and bring me the most gorgeous bric-a-brac you have there. Your husband also needs a "hubby corner," and because this master bedroom is large enough, let's fix him a special spot here near the front window." We moved a desk and a recliner from another room and hung some of his special plaques above his desk.

As I followed Mary Jo around, she taught me: The children's bedrooms should be next in importance (spend money for good mattresses, even if you have to wait for living room couches), followed by the dining room or kitchen, depending on where the family spends most of their mealtimes. She made sure my entry hall reflected emblems of our Christian faith.

Her team tackled our living room last. When they finished shoving the piano to another spot and repositioning couches and armchairs, we could actually seat more people. It was amazing.

I could hardly believe the new look they had created—at no expense to us and at no charge. I had often complained about our old furniture as "those awful hand-me-downs," since much of what we owned were relatives' cast-offs or used-furniture-store bargains. But now, in their new places near windows, those wonderful old wood grains shone as the sunlight bounced off of them.

When my husband came in from work and saw the transformation, he showed his pleasure by asking, "Does she do garages, too?" We laughed. In essence, we had a new house—a dream house, without buying a thing new.

Mary Jo's team of women is still busy some 25 years later, decorating other homes to the glory of God. And I'm still teaching writing lessons from time to time, because we all exercise our God-given gifts to help one another in the Body of Christ.

GOOD NIGHT, LORD

Lord, as I think back on that special day, I recognize that no matter where I ever move again—to a walk-up flat, a crude beach cottage, a cabin in the woods—I can decorate it to express our family's likes, tastes and personalities. Help me to continue to practice what Mary Jo taught me—that I don't have to spend a lot of money to create an attractive, pleasing house, and that from time to time I need to do an on-site inspection and ask, "Is Jesus pleased with this room?" Thank You for her team of women who gave so willingly of themselves to make us a happier family. May You Yourself reward them for their gift to us. Amen.

Full Circle

I have fought the good fight, I have finished the race, I have kept the faith.

2 TIMOTHY 4:7

Home again. But not really. After a 20-year absence, I'd been invited back to my "old" church as speaker for their women's retreat. What an honor! This was the church full of women who had mentored me when I was a mom with three young children.

I realized I had come full circle—now I was a grandmother coming to encourage a younger generation of women who love the Lord. I was plenty nervous.

At the last session on Sunday morning, I spoke on hospitality and mentoring. My definition for mentoring is short: Encourage and equip for excellence, passing down knowledge and training to one who is less experienced, helping that woman reach her full potential and do an even better job than me.

At our roundtable, I was surrounded by a few cherished "best friends" from years ago. During my speech, I paid them tribute and had each woman stand as I told what she had imparted to my life. Mary Jo had been my mentor for many years following that first day she came to decorate my house. Margaret made my curtains, taught one of my daughters how to sew and taught another to bake bread. Lib prayed faithfully with me every weekday morning for 17 years. Barbara had stood in some tough prayer gaps with me. Liz, owner of a flower boutique, had tried to teach me to arrange bouquets but was mostly my "let's have some fun" friend.

After I sat down and lunch was about to be served, a young woman came to our table and asked to speak to all of us "older" women. She said, "When we younger women, sitting at our table, heard how you have been friends all these years—even when one of you moved away—and how you have continued to pray for one another, it touched us all. We made a covenant today to do the same. We want to have lifelong friendships like you have had, and we want to pray for each other, too. Thank you for a great show-and-tell lesson." Most of us "oldies" shed a tear or two.

During this same visit, my husband and I went to our old home where we had lived from the time our children started school until they graduated. The new owners, friends of ours, were gracious to let us look around. The sticks our children planted were now gigantic trees. As I stood at the kitchen window and looked out, I remembered so many times I had stood there to watch a space launch. I especially remembered Apollo 14 because my 83-year-old granddaddy had come to watch it with us.

"Spectacular! Simply spectacular," he had said as we watched from the riverbank near our home. Just the day before we'd visited the Space Center's visitors' information building. Granddad and I stood gawking at the gray rock Neil Armstrong had brought back from his trip to the moon. It was locked tight under a glass dome for viewers to see but not touch. Granddaddy said it reminded him of the first time he'd seen an automobile at the turn of the century. Shaking his head, he remarked, "I remember as a child talking to men who carried bullets in them they had gotten while fighting for the Confederate Army. They let me play with their swords."

Now we are at the onset of the Third Millennium, and I consider myself blessed to be living at such a time as this. I'm glad I'm not living in my granddad's day. Or even in my mom's. Go back in time? No. Afraid of the future? Hopefully not. I've come full circle. While most of my parents' kin are gone, I have grandchildren to love and teach and encourage and mentor. I wouldn't miss this new millennium for the world.

As for going back home, the only home I want is right here where I live at the moment and the home Jesus has gone to prepare for me in heaven.

What about you? Have you come full circle, too? It doesn't matter in what season of your life you find yourself, God has some serendipities for you. And whatever trials you face, He will be there to help walk you through them.

GOOD NIGHT, LORD

Lord, we are a blessed generation. Thank You for all the ways You have brought us to this junction in life. Help us to fulfill the call You have given us in this brand-new century and new millennium. I pray in Jesus' name. Amen.

What's the Takeaway?

So teach us to number our days,
That we may present to Thee a heart of wisdom.

PSALM 90:12, NASB

An author is always conscious of the takeaway for the reader: What will she take away to apply to her life?

Pondering that thought recently, I considered a more eternal question: At the end of my life, what will others take away? Will I leave a legacy of bitterness, controversy or a judgmental attitude? Or will there be something positive and encouraging—something redeeming—to leave as a legacy?

What about you? Have you considered your sphere of influence? After all, no one else has the exact same circle of influence as you—the same friends, family members, extended family, coworkers.

Maybe you will ask yourself the questions I've been asking. Have I made amends to those who have been at odds with me? Have I been obedient to do what God has asked me to do?

David, the shepherd boy turned king, didn't die until he had fulfilled God's purpose for him in his generation (see Acts 13:36). That's what I'm trusting God to show me: how to complete His assigned task for me in my generation. Is that your desire, too? My all-time favorite card is titled "Just Think."

Just think,
you're not here by chance,
but by God's choosing.

His hand formed you

and made you

the person you are.

He compares you to no one else—

you are one of a kind.

You lack nothing

that His grace can't give you.

He has allowed you to be here

at this time in history

to fulfill His special purpose

for this generation.[1]

GOOD NIGHT, LORD

Lord, don't let me miss Your purpose for me. Let my life's takeaway be something the next generation will benefit from. Forgive me for the times when I have missed Your best. Now show me how to move forward in the things You would have me do. Knowing that You forgive me, I move ahead with no guilt or condemnation over what I've neglected. Let tomorrow be a new beginning in this area. I trust You to help me. Thank You, Lord. Amen.

Note

1. Roy Lessin, "Just Think." Used by permission of DaySpring® Cards.